Relationship Learning:
A Primer in Christian Education

RELATIONSHIP LEARNING

A PRIMER IN CHRISTIAN EDUCATION

C. Doug Bryan

BROADMAN PRESS
NASHVILLE, TENNESSEE

Unless otherwise stated, all Scripture quotations are from the *Revised Standard Version of the Bible*, copyrighted 1946, 1952, © 1971, 1973.

Library of Congress Cataloging-in-Publication Data

Bryan, C. Doug, 1954-
  Relationship Learning : a primer in Christian education / C. Doug
Bryan.
    p.   cm.
    ISBN: 0-8054-6016-0
      1. Christian education--Philosophy. 2. Interpersonal relations-
  -Religious aspects-Christianity. I. Title.
  BV1464.B793 1990
  268--dc20   90-30944
                                                                       CIP

With deep respect and appreciation,
this volume is dedicated to the faculty of the
School of Religious Education,
Southwestern Baptist Theological Seminary,
for their contributions to
Christian education.

Contents

Foreword

In *Relationship Learning: A Primer for Christian Education*, Doug Bryan welds together a most interesting summation of the historical, theological, and relational aspects of Christian education. Though the content is vast, the material is presented in a refreshingly new context. Intermingled within the body of the chapters are delightful learning exercises to be considered and experienced as the chapter unfolds. It is certainly a new approach to the study of traditional, historical, theological, and relational concerns of Christian education.

We are all aware that the field of Christian education takes place in a particular kind of context which is not only educative but also historical and theological. At the center of the religious education experience is a message, a mission, and a command from Christ to communicate the gospel. This communication takes place best when it is proffered within the Christian fellowship of *koinonia* and love. The communication is educative, to be sure, but it is practiced within a strong theological context of loving and fellowshiping believers.

Since the context of Christian education is strongly theological, it is imperative that the practice of Christian education discover its place in the history of the church. The resiliency of a discipline may be determined by its capability of withstanding the passing of time. Throughout church history, education has taken a formidable place alongside many other practices of the church. Christian education seemed to form a partnership with evangelism. As the church evangelized, close on the heels of evangelization was the establishment of

Christian education opportunities for the new converts to "grow in Christlikeness." Wherever church was practiced, education was practiced alongside conversion.

This book traces the development of historical educational practices. As the church established new missionary frontiers, educational frontiers likewise came into being. The process was hand-in-glove. One was never complete without the other, and they both complemented the other. As you read historically about the church, you will read about its educational penetration as well.

Education without theology is simply that: education. However, when it is coupled with theology, it becomes Christian in its nature and disciplining in its context. Education became the vehicle by which the early apostles and church fathers could effectively present the "new theology of the kingdom." Theology was best taught and preserved as it was communicated to the minds of believers in contexts that were conducive to learning, remembering, and practicing. Early in the teaching-learning process of the early church, teachers recognized that theology and doctrine were better learned when couched in educative models. The chapter that reflects theological considerations in the light of theology will provide different insights and learning.

After a convincing historical and theological presentation, Doug Bryan turns to the contents of Christian education. These contents are: A View of Christian Learning; Learner Characteristics and Faith Development Across the Life Span; Three Reflections of Christian Education: Family, Church, and School; and Christian Education Revealed in Stewardship.

Each of these four chapters presents a well-developed sequencing of the information you would expect to describe the involvement of education from a Christian perspective. When the learner is examined, the process surrounding the learner is unequivocally pedagogical while at the same time thoroughly Christian. You would likewise assume relational theological descriptions of the educational processes which enhance the characteristics of faith development as the education progresses through a Christian life span.

In a similar fashion, Bryan gives stimulating reflections of the three critical aspects of any Christian educative process—family, church, and school—as they interrelate in the development of the spiritual as well as physical and psychological ramifications of the learner. You will appreciate the sensitive manner in which this pivotal context is discussed.

The final chapter investigates Christian education revealed in stewardship. Here the words *stewardship* and *discipleship* are used in parallel expressions of a relationship with God. Stewardship in this context is the process of responsible living as the Christian gospel is internalized. Just having the gospel and keeping it is not acceptable: it must be lived out through a life and shared by that life with a lost and dying world. "For God so loved the world that he gave," so we must understand the depth of our stewardship of the gospel, our new life in Christ, and behave accordingly. Appreciation of this chapter will increase as you appropriate its information for yourself.

Christian education has been in need of a book of this nature. The book accomplishes a mammoth task of incorporation and interpolation, yet it is unpretentious in its presentation. Written from a crucible of practice in the church and with Christian learners, this book will become an outstanding source of motivation in the years ahead.

Jack D. Terry, Jr.
Dean, School of Religious Education
Southwestern Baptist Theological Seminary
Fort Worth, Texas

Introduction

Purpose

Relationship Learning: A Primer in Christian Education emerged from a concern with providing a basic understanding of the educational process in Christian education. Often, introductory courses in Christian education focus upon programming to the neglect of the theological, philosophical, historical, psychological, and sociological bases of the process. This book attempts to integrate the basic elements of Christian education into an introductory text.

Audience

The book is written with both the classroom teacher and the student in mind. The material covers the basic elements of Christian education. The instructors will supplement their classroom experiences with other materials they feel are more pertinent for immediate learning. The students will find this volume to be a general-summary approach to the different educational elements. Various learning activities are provided which should encourage and stimulate thinking. The work attempts to provoke both individual and group thought.

Presuppositions and Limitations

Each work begins with a number of presuppositions and limitations. Included in this volume are:

1. *All truth, wherever discovered, belongs to the Creator God.*— Truth discovered in psychology and other areas of human investiga-

tion belongs to God. Truth discovered in Scripture belongs to God. Wherever truth is found, God is the author.

2. *Integration is essential in the study of Christian education.*—Education is a broad discipline that must examine various contributions of other related disciplines. This work seeks to integrate the truth in Scripture and the truth found in other disciplines.

3. *This work is an introductory text.*—Only a broad panorama of Christian education has been depicted. Introductory texts cannot provide an in-depth treatment of any one element of Christian education.

4. *Christian education and learning are key elements in the process of discipleship.*—Whether it is termed discipleship, Christian growth, or sanctification, Christian education/learning is a vital element of Christian growth. Such growth can occur in both a formal and an informal setting.

5. *Those involved, either in their own spiritual growth or in leading the growth of others, have an inherent need to understand the basic process of Christian education.*—Broad implications exist for practitioners of Christian education from those in denominational publishing houses, to those serving in Christian foreign missions, and to the local Sunday School teacher.

6. *Christian education and other types of education often share similar elements.*—The differences for Christian education emerge from its theological and philosophical frame of reference. Learning that occurs in a Christian setting may contain elements identical to those in a non-Christian setting. Good learning is good learning, wherever it exists. Christian education/learning differs because its source or reference point is a personal relationship with Jesus Christ. Other aspects of the learning process are chosen and implemented in light of this relationship and scriptural teachings.

7. *Relationships form the core of all that is done in Christian education.*—Having begun in a faith relationship, we continue to teach, minister, and live out of that relationship. God is concerned with all of life's relationships. Christian education is learning to be rightly related to God, self, others, and the created order.

Overview

This work is divided into eight chapters. Chapters 1 and 2 deal with the historical backgrounds. Beginning with the biblical material and proceeding to the twentieth century, Christian education is viewed as discovering the Word and human beings' subsequent relational changes because of the Word. Chapter 3 provides an overview of the theological and philosophical elements crucial to a system of Christian education. Included is the author's own model for viewing the philosophical/educational questions. Chapter 4 provides an overview of various theories of learning. Included is an interpretation of the key elements in a theory of relationship learning.

Chapter 5 contains a life-span approach to the various development trends and changes from birth until death. Selected theorists and data are integrated into a relationship developmental theory of life. Christian education has a key role to play in the life of the individual. At each phase in life, Christian education can provide opportunities for individuals to experience fuller and richer relationships. Chapter 6 explores three reflections of Christian education: family, church, and school. Each of these institutions is examined with regard to its uniqueness. Guidelines for keeping the uniqueness of these institutions are provided.

Chapter 7 deals with stewardship, the end result of Christian education. Human relationships to God, self, others, and the created world are explored. Chapter 8 concludes with a model for viewing the world and specific plans for implementing Christian education opportunities in individual lives. Throughout the work, especially in the learning activities, focus has been given to stimulating thought and practice. The book ends by guiding individuals to assume responsibility for their own Christian education.

Evaluation

Any work is ultimately evaluated by its audience in light of the author's purpose and how the author fulfilled that purpose. If new insights are gained, if further study is encouraged, and if questions are raised, then the my purpose has been achieved. The remaining evaluations belong to the reader.

Part I:

Foundations for Christian Education

1
Historical Backgrounds for Christian Education: Biblical Period to the Renaissance

An Overview of the Relationship Theme

Created in the image of God, human beings experienced perfect relationship with God, themselves, others, and the created order. After the Fall, humans experienced broken relationships and began seeking ways to reestablish them. As the Chosen People, the Hebrews provided religious instruction through family education, the Sabbath, the festivals, and the holy days. Although God gave both the Law and the Prophets to direct humanity to God, human beings did not find restored relationships. The Word became flesh in the person of Jesus Christ who lived out His perfect relationship to God. Through a faith relationship in Christ, human beings can reestablish lost relationships with God, self, others, and the created order.

Inspired by God, men recorded the revelation of God in the Bible. The gospel through which men and women could find new life was recorded. The early church taught its members the Scriptures. With the collapse of the Roman Empire and the subsequent diminishing of education, both the laity and many of the clergy became ignorant of the Word. Superstition and ignorance flourished. A select few could read and had access to Scripture. Learning and Scripture were preserved in European monasteries and cathedral schools. However, few received an education. Only briefly in isolated parts of Western Europe and in the Eastern Roman Empire did learning flourish. For the vast multitudes, the Word was lost because of illiteracy and few copies of available Scripture.

The Crusades opened Western eyes to the riches of the East and especially to the precious ancient manuscripts. A revitalization of learning occurred. Out of cathedral schools, which sought to preserve learning for a special few, universities emerged. These early universities promoted the study of the ancient writings. While a few individuals were encouraged to study, the great majority were unaffected by the growth and development of learning institutions. Various groups, such as the Brethren of the Common Life and the Lollards, provided opportunity for all to have access to God through the study of Scripture. Slowly the Word of God was becoming once again the Word of and for the people.

Those living in the progressive, technological twentieth century pride themselves on their enlightened sophistication. Rapid advancements are made each day in varied fields of study. In fact, what is learned today may become obsolete or replaced in the near future. We know more today than any other generation. However, according to E. D. Hirsch, Jr., in his best-seller *Cultural Literacy: What Every American Needs to Know,* "Only two thirds of the citizens in the United States are literate."[1] Why? How can we be so knowledgeable, yet so illiterate? Hirsch refers to cultural literacy, which involves the acquiring of needed knowledge in order to function effectively within the context of a given society. This knowledge allows us to communicate effectively within our own culture.

What does cultural literacy have to do with a book on Christian education? As a college professor, I have become increasingly cognizant of the lack of historical and cultural knowledge among college students. Basic knowledge about our history and heritage is lacking among the present and future makers of history.

If there is a lack in secular education in transmitting our historical heritage, what about the knowledge regarding our own Christian heritage? Various questions can illustrate this lack of understanding. What is the Shema? What can we learn from Jesus' practice of education? How did the early Christians regard public education? What is the relationship between the modern university and the church? What did the great Reformers contribute to modern education? What was the original intent of the modern Sunday School movement? What was the relationship between the Sunday School and nineteenth-century American life?

History can help answer these questions. From the answers, we can make intelligent decisions about our present Christian educational system. The responsibility for "not knowing" does not lie entirely with the student. Rather, those given the responsibility of teaching are accountable for the transmission of the Christian message. As Jesus commanded His disciples to go and teach, our teaching should involve the sharing of historical achievements and development.

Various reasons exist for studying history. History provides a new perspective and humility on our place in world history. Studying history can illuminate some of our past errors and show the complexities of our own development. Marcus Tullius Cicero (106-43 B.C.), the Roman statesman, wrote, "Not to know the events which happened before one was born, that is to remain always a boy." Studying history allows us not to be confined to the present but to expand and grow as we acknowledge our legacy from previous generations (See Figure 1.1).

In these first two chapters, the history of Christian education is presented not out of a sense of tradition or obligation, but rather because of its timely significance. As we question what we should be doing "educationally," we can gain insight by looking at our historical roots. In fact, we may realize that some of the practices of today are the consequences of historical and cultural choices made by previous generations. Such study may enable us to evaluate current practices and to determine if new practices are needed that will communicate God's Word to the present generation.

From the onset, the reader should be aware of several basic premises, limitations, and intentions. It is not possible to present a comprehensive history of Christian education in this volume. What the reader will find are brief glimpses into important phases of growth and development. Hopefully, appetites will be aroused; further study will

CHRISTIAN EDUCATION
AN OVERVIEW

**Here and Now
(Chapter Eight)**

**Christian Education Revealed in Stewardship
(Chapter Seven)**

**Three Reflections of Christian Education:
Family, Church, and School
(Chapter Six)**

**Learner Characteristics & Faith Development
Across the Lifespan
(Chapter Five)**

**A Christian View of Learning
(Chapter Four)**

PART TWO: TOWARD A PRACTICE OF CHRISTIAN EDUCATION

PART ONE: FOUNDATIONS FOR CHRISTIAN EDUCATION

Historical Backgrounds (Chapters 1-2)	**Theological and Philosophical Foundations (Chapter 3)**

Figure 1.1

be encouraged. Second, the history will be largely that of the church in the West as it moved to the shores of the New World. Third, I will attempt to show how various educational practices arose out of given cultural and social contexts. Fourth, I hope the work will cause the reader to think and to examine lessons of the past for present and future application value. To accomplish this end, various activities and questions will be used. Finally, studying history can provide a sense of continuity with the past and reveal the pivotal point we have in relationship to future generations. We are heirs to the past and provide a legacy to the future.

We live in a day that demands critical teaching as we move from the twentieth to the twenty-first century of Christianity. Throughout history, various periods have emphasized different aspects of teaching in relationship to the Christian faith. At times, the flame of learning was very bright; at other times, the flame was almost extinguished. Fortunately, the light and its accompanying vision have been caught, kindled, and transmitted throughout history. For the light of Christian learning and influence to be conveyed, a model based upon our understanding of the past, as well as the present, is needed.

Old Testament

Calling the Chosen People

Teaching and learning are at the heartbeat of God's message for His creation. Genesis 1:26-28 records:

> Then God said, "Let us make man in our image, after our likeness; and let them have dominion over the fish of the sea, and over the birds of the air, and over the cattle, and over all the earth, and over every creeping thing that creeps upon the earth." So God created man in his own image, in the image of God he created him; male and female he created them. And God blessed them, and God said unto them, "Be fruitful and multiply, and fill the earth and subdue it; and have dominion over the fish of the sea and over the birds of the air and over every living thing that moves upon the earth."

While this passage may seem familiar, it needs to be examined from a new perspective. How does humankind have dominion over the created order as God has commanded? In order to exert dominion properly, one must exert good stewardship. Stewardship involves honestly knowing and appraising what one has and then acting in accordance with that best knowledge. What an excellent way of viewing teaching and learning! We must know, and then we must act on that knowledge. Responsible living demands living responsibly with our fellow creatures. God's intent for human beings is that they be found faithful, stewards who acknowledge their Creator in life and service. Teaching and learning are a part of our pilgrimage as God's stewards.

Throughout history, God has used various institutions, rituals, and people to instruct humanity in His ways. As God fellowshiped with Adam and Eve, He gave them commandments to follow. Rather than being punitive or restrictive, the teachings established the needed freedom and direction necessary for fellowship with the Creator. In the garden, God commanded that they should eat of every tree except the tree of the knowledge of good and evil (Gen. 2:15-17). Educators today acknowledge the importance of establishing limits in rearing children. God fathered the new creation and set limits upon humankind not to restrict but to allow people to grow and to reach full maturity. Like children, Adam and Eve violated their commanded limits. Consequently, the first couple was driven from the garden and compelled to till the earth. However, the Creator's message continued to be taught to His creation.

Various examples illustrate God's concern for His created order's struggle to regain the lost fellowship. God demonstrated His desire for a worthy sacrifice in the different offerings of Cain and Abel, two brothers (Gen. 4:3-7). When Cain slew Abel, God again taught humankind the importance of human life (Gen. 4:8-16). Cain lived with a mark that set him apart. The stigma would teach the young world of the importance of living in harmony. It would also show the seriousness of taking the life of what God has created—one's fellow human being.

While God watched the progression or regression of His creation, He witnessed a vicious cycle of disobedience, punishment, repentance, obedience, and again disobedience. While human beings sought to find their lives, they lost them as they became slaves to their own desires. Later the world became so sinful that God destroyed it, but He spared one righteous man and his family (Gen. 6:5-22).

After such a dramatic display of God's deliverance and power, Noah's descendants would surely obey. Rather than obeying God, the people chose to become "gods" themselves by constructing a great tower to reach the heavens. God intervened and caused division among the language of the people (Gen. 11:9). Humanity's great accomplishment and human attempts to gain a name for themselves became the Tower of Babel. Humankind was dispersed throughout the world, again seeking what was lost—perfect fellowship with God. Unfortunately, humans turned to various indulgences of the flesh and constructed various pagan deities to fill the emptiness in their lives.

God chose one of Noah's descendants, Abraham, to make His will known to the scattered peoples of the earth. Called by God, Abraham left his family and journeyed as directed by God (Gen. 12:1-4). Being an old man without children by his wife Sarah, Abraham nevertheless believed God faithful. Advanced in years, Sarah bore Abraham a son known as Isaac (Gen. 21:1-3). After Abraham showed his faithfulness and willingness to offer his only son as a sacrifice to God, God said to Abraham, "By myself I have sworn, says the Lord, because you have done this, and have not withheld your son, your only son, I will indeed bless you, and I will multiply your descendants as the stars of heaven and as the sand which is on the seashore. And your descendants shall possess the gate of their enemies, and by your descendants shall all the nations of the earth bless themselves, because you have obeyed my voice" (Gen. 22:16-8). From Isaac, twin sons, Jacob and Esau, would be born (Gen. 25:19-26). From Jacob, the sons that would eventually be known as the sons of Abraham or twelve tribes of Israel would descend.

These examples reveal that early in our history God sought to reestablish a relationship with His creation. Each relationship involved obedience to God. These relationships show human need for God's limits and directions for growth and development. When humanity failed to be obedient to God, the relationship suffered. As the relational God, He calls for humans to find life in fellowship with Him. As God's people multiplied, the need to share principles of improved relationship became more and more important.

The clearest example of the importance of teaching in the Old Testament may be found in the giving of the Ten Commandments to the children of Israel. The descendants of Abraham had been living in Egyptian captivity for a number of years. While their identity had been maintained, outside cultural and religious influences, like the Egyptian deities, had affected their character. Rather than exclusive devotion to Yahweh, the Hebrews also practiced Egyptian idol worship.

After a dramatic rescue from Pharaoh and while Moses was receiving the law on Mount Sinai, the people reverted to pagan practices and pleaded with Aaron to construct a golden calf for worship (Ex. 32:1-4). In their hearts, they still had not learned the exclusive allegiance required of those who believe in the one true God. In their desperation, the Hebrews turned to the graven images they had known in Egyptian captivity. While God judged those who turned from relationship with Him (Ex. 32:35), He continued in His covenant with His people.

In the Ten Commandments, instructions were granted for one's relationship with God and with one's fellow human beings. Rather than being restrictive, the Commandments were intended to teach a young nation the character of God. These Commandments reveal the nature of God and the consequent life-style of those who seek to reflect or imitate that sacred nature. A part of what humanity sought was slowly being revealed to the Chosen People. From this highlighted summary of the forming of the young Hebrew nation, attention must now be given to the educational practices of this nation that was to become a nation of priests to the world.

Learning Activity 1.1

1. Review the creation account found in Genesis. Meditate upon the passage. What does the passage reveal about the nature of the human race?
2. Life is a cycle of "obedience, disobedience, punishment, repentance, obedience, etc." Do you agree or disagree? Why?
3. Examine the Ten Commandments. Paraphrase the Commandments.
4. Review each of the Ten Commandments and write positive consequences of each Commandment.

Preexilic Period

To comprehend the depth and scope of Hebrew education, one must remember that education was essentially religious in nature. This religious nature included two levels: an individual righteousness to God through personal faith and obedience and a corporate identity as the kingdom of priests—the Chosen People. These concepts are found in Deuteronomy 6:4-9 and Deuteronomy 11:18-21. Deuteronomy 6:4-9, the Shema, represents Israel's call to instruct her children in the ways of God. (Detailed analysis of the Shema will be given later.) For the Hebrews, religion and education were synonymous. Instruction in the ways of God was a part of the daily life of the Hebrews. The "Torah," "The Law," or "The Teaching" describes what is customary in education and religion.[2]

Various mechanisms were set into motion that would help preserve religious identity. The Hebrews were commanded not to intermarry, thus preserving national unity. Definite commandments were given to promote a high degree of personal integrity and harmonious ethical relationships. Four groups of people took responsibility for promoting these ends. They were parents, priests, sages, and prophets.

Parents.—The responsibility for education as outlined in the Shema rested initially with the family. Both mother and father instructed their children. Survival in a primitive and nomadic society demanded vocational training. In addition to basic religious instruction, the father taught the son a vocational skill, and the mother taught the daughter skills in homemaking.[3] This vocational training was aimed at preparing the child to assume adult responsibility within the society. Learning survival skills was crucial, not only to survival of the individual but also to the survival of the larger community. Prior to becoming a literate society, much of this instruction was oral and by imitation. In the family's instructions, repetition and memorization were heavily stressed.

A family-centered approach to learning emerged. The Hebrews viewed the birth of a child as favor before God. Children were highly regarded, and, consequently, concerted effort was given to the training of children. Various rituals emerged which were employed as opportunities to teach children about particularly significant religious truths. Curiosity about rituals provoked questions which provided teaching opportunities concerning religious significance attached to those rituals.

Rituals included circumcision of the male on the eighth day of life. Forty days following the birth of child, the family offered a burnt offering and a sin offering at the Temple. When the male reached thirteen years, a special ceremony, the Bar Mizvah, marked his coming to the age of legal responsibility as Son of the Commandment. Parents also used the Sabbath, the festivals, and the holy days as teaching opportunities. The Hebrews discovered the importance of imitation and symbols in the educative process. Rituals and ceremony became a time of expressing unity as a community and of communicating deeper messages concerning the nature and character of God.

Various symbols emerged which encouraged the teaching and the learning of the young children. For example, several articles of clothing were intended to remind the wearer and the observer of God and the Commandments. The male wore a tallith, or prayer shawl, to remind himself and others of the need of personal righteousness before God. A zizit, a braided ropelike tie, had a gold color to represent glory to God and a blue color to represent personal righteousness. Phylacteries, boxes made of goat skin containing portions of Scripture, were tied to the forehead and arm. These elements reminded the wearer and the observer of spiritual truths.

Priests.—Teaching responsibility was shared by the priests, sages, and prophets. The priests, from the tribe of Levi, provided information to the people regarding the will and nature of God. In Deuteronomy 33:8-10, the duties of the priests are outlined. The priests led in worship. Each sacrifice, symbol, and ceremony provided the vehicle for conveying a devotion to God and for instructing beliefs about God. Sacrifices proclaimed and portrayed the nature of God and conveyed His holiness, our sinfulness, the need for repentance and faithful obedience. The priests provided the public instruction needed for the people of God.[4]

Sages.—Another group of instructors consisted of the wise men, or sages. Old Testament history gives little information on this group. Prior to the time of Saul, only the Book of Job mentions the sages. Although more prominent after the exile, these men did teach in earlier times. Because of their age and experience, they were respected members of the community. Their purpose was instructing in wisdom that involved reference to God. They praised such virtues as truth, justice, patience, humility, and godliness. Giving special attention to the young, they hoped to lead youth to godly maturity.[5]

Prophets.—In the context of a world in depravity, the prophets arose to be spokesmen for God. Through public speaking and addresses, these prophets challenged the people with God's message. By proclaiming the need for a contrite heart and faithful obedience, the prophets condemned religious ritualism that was devoid of genuine devotion. These spokesmen directed the attention of the people to the nature and character of God for daily life. Denouncing sin, these prophets proclaimed the need for repentance, faith, and obedience. In the time of Elijah and Elisha, the prophets were organized into communities.[6]

Learning Activity 1.2

1. In the preexilic period, there were four groups involved in teaching. Match each group with the appropriate letter.

      _____ 1. Sages   A. vocational skills

      _____ 2. Priests   B. spokesmen for genuine obedience

      _____ 3. Prophets   C. led in temple worship

      _____ 4. Parents   D. counsel youth on the virtues of the godly life

Postexilic Education

The Babylonian captivity brought lifelong changes to the Hebrews. In this time of disgrace and captivity, the Hebrews learned valuable lessons. Noted Bible teacher, H. I. Hester listed seven benefits of the exile for the Jews: (1) thoroughly cured of idolatry; (2) development of the synagogue; (3) collected literature; (4) the spiritual and personal emphasis of religion; (5) appreciation for the Law of Moses; (6) unity in ideals and purposes; and (7) appreciation of their destiny as a nation.[7]

After the Babylonian exile in 586 B.C. and the return to Jerusalem, dramatic changes occurred in Hebrew education. In Babylonia, exiled Jews had been exposed to an advanced and literate culture. With this new exposure, the world awareness of the Hebrews changed. The exiled people realized that a loss of identity would occur if measures were not taken to ensure their identity as a people. Education was one means of assuring both a religious and a national identity.

After the destruction of the temple in 586 B.C., the synagogue developed as a place of worship and study. Upon returning to their homeland, the people recognized a need to return to the Law and to become a people of the Book. Whereas education had been primarily of an oral tradition, the focus shifted to an emphasis on reading and writing. Of primary importance were the Torah (the first five books of the Law) and the Talmud (the interpretation of the Torah). During this period, several writings were produced, such as Job, Proverbs,

and Ecclesiastes. Education now began to be built around the synagogue. Synagogues developed wherever ten adult Jewish men were
present. Even after the rebuilding of the Temple under Zerubbabel's
leadership, the synagogues continued.

Simple in structure, the traditional synagogue was a rectangular auditorium with a raised speaker's platform. Behind the raised platform
was a portable chest or shrine housing Old Testament scrolls. While
the rulers or elders sat facing the congregation, the congregation sat
along two or three walls and on mats, stone benches, or wooden
chairs. The speaker would stand when reading the Scriptures and
would sit when preaching. Everyone stood for prayer.

The synagogue service had definite order and ritual. The elements
of worship were similar to that found in twentieth-century synagogues
and churches. A typical worship service included: an antiphonal reci-
tation of the Shema and the Shemone Esreh (a series of praises to
God), prayer, singing of psalms unaccompanied by music, readings
from the Old Testament law and prophets, a sermon, and a benediction. During the week, the synagogue was multipurpose in function. It
became a center for the education of Jewish males, study of the Old
Testament, administration of law, holding of political meetings, and
services for the dead.[8]

After returning from the Babylonian captivity, the Jewish leaders
became increasingly aware of the importance of formal education. In
A.D. 64, High Priest Joshua ben Gamala issued an ordinance that
instituted a system of elementary schools for boys in each district and
town.[9] The synagogues were taller than other buildings to emphasize
the importance of God's teaching. The Beth Ha-Shepher, "House of
the Book," gave emphasis to the study of the Torah for boys beginning
at age five. Beth Ha-Shepher was commonly held in the synagogue
and attendance was compulsory. Aramaic had become the spoken
vernacular; however, because the Torah was written in Hebrew, its
study necessitated the study of reading and writing Hebrew.

After learning the Hebrew alphabet, the student committed large
portions of Scripture to memory. At this elementary school level, a

minimum amount of memorized Scripture was expected. Five passages constituted this requirement: the Shema (Deut. 6:4-9); the Hallel (Ps. 113—118); the story of creation (Gen. 1—5); the essence of Levitical law (Lev. 1—8); and a personal text that began with the first letter of the child's name and ended with the last letter of his name.[10]

In the structure of the synagogue, all Jewish males became students of the Law. Instruction occurred under the supervision of the synagogue scribe. Older males went on to study the Torah and the Oral Torah or Mishnah. At the age of sixteen, gifted males associated themselves with rabbinical teachers. In this phase, an intellectual exchange of ideas occurred between the student and teacher.

Religious Classes and Sects.—Various classes developed that further encouraged the growth of education. Three groups identified by the Jewish historian Josephus were the Sadducees, Pharisees, and the Essenes. The Sadducees were a small group of wealthy laymen. Chiefly, they were landowners who were both highly influential and highly ritualistic. The Sadducees did not see a need for additional commentaries on the Torah. Most of their activity centered around the temple.[11]

The Pharisees, a layman's group of middle-class origins, wished to withdraw from everything unclean or sinful. They stressed submission to the will of Yahweh, even in the face of injustice and possible persecution. While the Pharisees believed in the bodily resurrection of the dead, they discounted the expectation of a violent and universal upheaval in the last day. Whereas the Sadducee's chief activity was in the temple, the Pharisee's primary center of activity was in the synagogues. Possessing a keen interest in social concerns, the Pharisees were active throughout the Dispersion because of their willingness to accept existing political authorities. The Pharisees believed that both the Torah and traditions were binding. It is interesting to note that the Apostle Paul was a Pharisee.[12]

The agent and assistants of the Pharisees were the professional lawyers, or scribes. These teachers exerted significant influence in Jewish education. With admission open to all classes of people, the scribes were the learned and legal class of the day. In addition to teaching the law, the scribes interpreted its meaning. Schools of scribes came to be known as rabbinical schools. The leaders of these schools were known as rabbis. Gradually, these rabbis became recognized authorities over the religious and educational life of the nation.[13]

Theoretically the scribes were teachers without pay. Ideally, they had a trade by which to support themselves.[14] The scribes produced the Haggadah and Halakah. The Haggadah was a manual for observing the feasts on holy days. The Halakah contained legal decisions that were binding on the conscience. Held in high esteem, scribes played a part in the great Sanhedrin: a religious and legislative body whose concern was biblical commentary, universal education, the rights of women, and proper procedures for courts of law.[15]

A smaller group of approximately four thousand were the Essenes, a strict religious sect. Becoming an Essene involved a two-to-three-year probationary period and the pledging of personal property and wealth into a common fund. The Essenes surpassed the Pharisees in their legalism. Their basic thrust was to withdraw from society. In fact, they did not offer animal sacrifices in Jerusalem because they regarded the temple as defiled and corrupted by her priests. As a symbol of their own purity and intent, they wore white robes.[16]

Religious Observances.—Various religious duties and practices by the Hebrews sought to maintain communion with God. Prayer was an essential aspect of the religious life with prayers offered in the mornings, afternoons, and evenings. Before and after meals, a prayer of thanksgiving for food was made. When reciting morning prayers, individuals wore phylacteries to remind them of the importance of keeping God's commandments. Individuals were expected to have appointed times during the week to study the Torah. Various observances on the Sabbath and the festivals were strictly followed.[17]

The Sabbath, the seventh day of the week, commemorated the day of rest commanded by God. Beginning on Friday evening and ending at Saturday evening, the Jewish Sabbath was a time of both rest and celebration. Individuals wore special clothes and refrained from work.

Meals consisted of special foods. However, more than rest and special foods, the Sabbath was a day of special study of the Torah. The entire family spent the Friday evening meal together. Later, they joined others to study the Torah at the house of study. In time, it became customary to hold communal services in the synagogue on Friday nights.[18]

Additional educational and worship experiences involved major festivals, the high holy days and minor holy days. Initially, the festivals were agricultural in origin, though later, they achieved a strong religious significance for the Jewish people. These festivals not only marked the agricultural year but also the historical workings of God in the lives of the Chosen People.

The first major festival is *Pesach,* or the Passover (Ex. 12:1-28). This festival, observed in the spring and marking the barley harvest, signifies the deliverance of the Hebrew slaves from Egyptian captivity. Oldest of the Jewish festivals, Pesach is the festival of redemption. The second major festival is *Shovuos* or Pentecost (Ex. 23:16; Lev. 23:15-22). Observed in the summer and marking the wheat harvest, Shovuos celebrates the giving of the law on Mount Sinai. The last of the three major festivals is *Sukkos* or the Festival of the Tabernacles (Lev. 23:40-44). Sukkos, observed in the fall and marking the grape harvest, celebrates the forty years of wandering in the wilderness and involves a harvest-thanksgiving festival. All of these festivals are ones of celebration and instruction. They remind the participants of God's gracious gift of life and redemption.

Two high holy days exist among those of the Jewish faith. The first is *Yom Kippur,* or the Day of Atonement. Yom Kippur includes fasting and repentance. Occurring five days from Sukkos, this day marks the end of the old year. Rosh Hashanah, also known as the Day of Judgment, is the beginning of the Jewish New Year. Rather than revelry, Rosh Hashanah involves approaching the New Year with a contrite heart. This holy day involves repenting of bad actions, asking for God's mercy, and performing good deeds.

Three minor holy days are observed. The first is Tishoh B' Ov, or the ninth day of the Jewish month of Ov. This day is one of mourning for the destruction of the temple and Jerusalem. It is a day of fasting. The second day is Hanukkah, or the Festival of Lights. This is a day of great celebration in which the Jews commemorate the successful revolt of Judas Maccabee of the Hasmonean family against Antiochus Epiphanes. The third is Purim, or the Feast of Esther, which celebrates the deliverance of the Persian Jews from their enemy, Haman. Purim is described in the Book of Esther.

Learning Activity 1.3

1. The Jewish people held special observances on the Sabbath. List special observances and practices that characterize how you spend the Lord's Day.
2. Outline the major Jewish festivals and holy days. List their agricultural significance (where appropriate) and religious significance.
3. What are the special observances that your church has during the year? Describe the significance. Which ones have special meaning to you?
4. What is your most memorable Christmas or Easter celebration? Explain.
5. What are the key ingredients in a special religious observation?

New Testament

Jesus

The New Testament builds on the educational groundwork established in the Old Testament. The greatest Teacher of humankind, Jesus Christ, clearly reflected His Jewish educational upbringing. Jesus' parents gave Him religious as well as vocational instruction.

Scripture gives a few glimpses into the early life and religious teaching of Jesus. Luke 2:21 reveals His circumcision on the eighth day. Luke 2:22-24 documents Mary's purification and the offering of the dove. Luke 2:41-48 records Jesus' visit to Jerusalem where He as-

JEWISH FESTIVALS AND HOLY DAYS

Jewish Festivals and Holy Days

Three Major Jewish Festivals

Pesach (Passover) (Exodus 12:1–28)	marks the beginning of the barley harvest (spring)	God's deliverance of the Hebrew slaves
Shovuos (Pentecost) (Exodus 23:16; Leviticus 23:15–22)	marks the beginning of the wheat harvest (summer)	God gives the Law at Mount Sinai
Sukkos (Leviticus 23:40–44)	marks the beginning of the grape festival (fall)	Forty years of wandering in the wilderness

---

Two High Holy Days

Yom Kippur (Day of Atonement)	fasting and repentance; marks the end of the old year
Rosh Hashanah (Day of Judgment)	repentance and performing good deeds; marks the new year

---

Three Minor Holy Days

Tishoh B'ov	day of mourning for the destruction of the temple and Jerusalem
Hanukkah (Festival of Lights)	commemorates the successful revolt against Antiochus Epiphanes
Purim (Feast of Esther)	commemorates the deliverance of the Persian Jews from their enemy, Haman

For further study see Schauss, *The Jewish Festivals*

Figure 1.2

tounded the temple leaders with His knowledge. In regard to spiritual growth and social growth, Luke 2:52 records, "Jesus increased in wisdom and in stature, and in favor with God and man."

Jesus is the Teacher after whom all Christians should model their lives. Jesus focused His ministry on teaching and training. Noted Christian educator J. M. Price wrote:

> Jesus saw in teaching the supreme opportunity for shaping the ideals, attitudes, and conduct of people. He was not primarily an orator, reformer, or ruler, but rather a teacher. To be sure, he did not belong to the professional class of scribes and rabbis who give minute interpretations of the law, but he taught.[19]

In at least forty-five instances in the four Gospels, Jesus is referred to as teacher, not preacher.[20] In John 13:13, Jesus said, "You call me Teacher and Lord; and you are right, for so I am."

In public education, one maxim is to place the best teacher with the most difficult and "unreachable" student. The disadvantaged, the unmotivated, and less-gifted learners need the best of the teaching corps. That is precisely what God did. People had continually failed to respond to the Law and the Prophets. God sent Himself Incarnate to seek and to instruct a group of undisciplined, unmotivated, and selfish people. The Best was sent to reach and teach the worst.

Scripture records Jesus' teaching in the synagogues. Typically two synagogue services were conducted on the Sabbath. The morning worship was preaching; the afternoon service was primarily teaching. Jesus probably taught in the synagogues in the afternoon services.[21] In addition to the more formal aspects of teaching, Jesus' life displayed informal teaching. Using the everyday occurrences of life, Jesus talked about the nature of God. He taught in a wide variety of such occurrences: when He was thirsty, He instructed the woman at the well; facing religious criticism, He associated with the sinful; and rejoicing in the interruption of children, He taught of the childlike qualities of faith.

Jesus gave instruction in both large and small-group settings. However, the small group illustrated the dynamics and the full intent of His teaching. In these groups, Jesus gave more in-depth answers to what had been asked. Truly, those who sought His leadership, who hungered and thirsted after "righteousness" (Matt. 5:6), found fulfillment. The Word became priority for them. Small-group teaching allowed for individual involvement and for the creation of action plans for a new life-style. Following the crucifixion, resurrection, and ascension of Jesus, those He taught in small groups were empowered by the Holy Spirit, and they were the first to herald the "gospel" or "good news" to the world.

Jesus employed a variety of teaching methods, including the use of objects, dramatics, stories, parables, lectures, and questions. According to C. B. Eavey:

> He used in essence practically all the methods common in teaching since His day and He used them most effectively, teaching as no other has ever taught. As a master-teacher, He made it a practice to adapt Himself to the situation and to the state and need of the one or ones taught. Thus, while He used methods, He was above method in the formal sense of the word.[22]

Several observations should be made regarding Jesus' methodology. While there is nothing "extraordinary" in any one method, several principles are noteworthy. First, Jesus employed variety. No one method would attract and sustain the interest of all learners. Variety allows for reaching a wider range of learners. The only poor method is one that is used exclusively. Second, Jesus chose those objects and parables that were in keeping within the experiences of His listeners, such as agricultural, commercial, and homemaking illustrations. Third, Jesus chose the simplest language to convey great spiritual truths. Using language common to His hearers, He communicated effectively to those willing to listen. Language was not to confuse truth, but to convey truth.

To discover the effectiveness of Jesus' teaching, one should not look exclusively to methodology. The greatest rewards will be found in the philosophical assumptions of Jesus. This philosophy is not one that has been articulately recorded in words, rather the philosophy has been recorded in Christ's life. His secret was love and acceptance.

This secret may be found in Jesus' personality and attitude toward humankind. Jesus taught through His personality, which reflected discipline, acceptance, and acknowledgment of who He was and His mission. Jesus found acceptance and approval with the Father through obedience. Out of this acceptance, Jesus developed the ability to love, to accept, and to reach out to others. He sought to impart more than factual knowledge. He desired that His listeners have spiritual prosperity. Jesus saw the fulfillment of human potential through finding the right relationship with the Father. Through a believing and living faith as revealed through Jesus Christ, human beings, in their struggle for the missing relationship, would find perfect satisfaction. Jesus' love attracted others and would eventually conquer the world. Although there would be suffering, even death could not conquer the love of God.

In summary, the teaching ideal of Jesus must not be overlooked or minimized, as is the temptation, when we become involved in the educative process. In our attempts to achieve a high degree of educational sophistication and reputation, we may lose sight of the goal of Jesus. Rather than seeking to build great kingdoms or structures of education, educators should not overlook the importance of the solitary life that finds a place of service in God's kingdom. A vital spiritual quality exists in education. When education, whether secular or Christian, seeks to regard itself as a means to only material gain and prosperity, an emptiness or shallowness becomes readily apparent.

Educational historian, Frederick Mayer wrote:

> All of this is extremely important in education. We preach spirituality and respect for the individual, yet most of the time we are so concerned about buildings, equipment, and other material considerations, that we neglect the teacher and the student. We provide for the comforts of the body, but we neglect the welfare of the soul. We look upon laboratories and stadiums as signs of progress, when they may only

hide an empty spirit. We do not know the core of education; thus, many of our institutions of higher learning are centers of organized confusion.[23]

While Mayer was writing in a history of secular education, the same idea may be applied to our present attempts at Christian education.

Learning Activity 1.4

1. Read a selected Gospel account and examine the characteristics of Jesus. Write the characteristics and the references.
2. What do you consider to be the significant ideas about Jesus's teaching?

Paul

The second most important teaching personality in the New Testament is the apostle Paul. As the central teaching leader in the New Testament church, Paul's background gives an excellent illustration of one who experienced the best of Jewish education. Paul was a Pharisee by both birth and conviction (Acts 23:5-6; Phil. 3:5). He was taught by Gamaliel, a renowned Jewish teacher (Acts 22:3). In addition to his excellent religious training, Paul received vocational training as a tentmaker (Acts 18:3).

Following his conversion and before beginning his missionary work, Paul spent approximately ten years in training (Gal. 1:15-24). Although he was an early persecutor of the church, Paul became a great missionary for that church. Interestingly, the great intellect and enthusiasm that Paul had prior to his conversion, he later employed in his Christian life. This keen mind and systematic thinker became the leading voice as the church penetrated the Gentile world. Paul taught in a variety of settings: synagogues, the riverside, Mars Hill, a school, a market place, the theater, the home, ships, the courthouse, and even the prison. Like Jesus, Paul taught through a number of methods: lecture, debate, discussions, show and tell, team teaching, self-study, and writing. Through his writings, Paul supplied the world with an excellent discussion of Christian truth.

Chosen by God, Paul became the leading spokesman for the gospel as it ventured into a highly articulate Gentile culture. Steeped in a long history of Greek philosophy, the Roman Empire was highly literate. Paul was an early Christian apologist, one who made an intellectual defense of the gospel. Through his writings and teachings, Paul helped the gospel achieve intellectual and literary credibility. In addition, Paul continued to aid Christian understanding of the message of Christ in a complex and hostile world. Guided by the Holy Spirit, Paul provided instruction for daily life, as well as church life and practice. Through the Scriptures recorded by Paul and other New Testament writers, all the world can hear and learn of the gospel message. Through the Holy Spirit, this written Word can become living Word.

Church History

Early Church

In the newly developing church, five kinds of teaching existed: Christian interpretation of the Hebrew Scriptures, teaching of the gospel, an emphasis upon commitment to Christ, an emphasis upon the life and teachings of Jesus, and teaching ethical choices which Christians faced.[24] The early Christians were involved in three types of meetings: (1) meetings of prayer, hymn singing, reading of the apostolic letters, teaching, and prophecy; (2) the common meal followed by the Lord's Supper; and (3) business meetings. In the early church, instruction and worship were closely intertwined.[25]

Two rituals or observances in the early church were baptism and the Lord's Supper. Christian baptism signified initiation into the community of faith. It had its origins in the Old Testament act of ritual purification and proselyte baptism. As an act of obedience, baptism symbolizes the believer's faith in the life, death, burial, and resurrection of Jesus Christ. Romans 6:1-4 provides an understanding of the New Testament concept of baptism. *The Didache*, or *Teaching of the Apostles*, was an early church manual, teaching a tri-immersion in the name of the Father, Son, and Holy Spirit. However, *The Didache* permits baptism by affusion (pouring) if insufficient water is available. Until the end of the fifth century, normal church baptism was adult baptism.[26]

Early observance of the Lord's Supper was possibly a fellowship meal in which Jesus' actions with the bread were repeated at the beginning of the meal. At the end of the meal, Jesus' words with the cup were repeated. Throughout church history, various interpretations emerged regarding baptism and the Lord's Supper. It is beyond the scope of this work to go into such treatment. However, the reader is encouraged to explore the changes and the meanings behind these two central expressions of Christian church life.

Since the early church was located in Palestine and was comprised almost entirely of Jewish members, observation of the Sabbath continued. Jewish Christians continued to attend the synagogues and participate in the Jewish religious practices. When Gentiles joined the church and as persecution against Christians increased, changes occurred. One of the great battles of the early church concerned whether one first had to become a Jew in terms of Jewish religious tradition in order to become a Christian. Paul fought to prevent an attempt to "Judaize" the Christian faith and the newly converted Gentile Christians. In time the church decided that Gentiles converted to Christianity did not have to follow Jewish religious observances.

Jewish Christians continued to meet in the synagogue until they were forced to leave. The observance of the Lord's Supper was conducted on Saturday evenings—the beginning of Sunday (Acts 20:7). Under Emperor Trajan, it appears that evening gatherings became illegal, and the meetings were moved to early Sunday morning. Gradually, the link with the Jewish Sabbath was broken, and Christians celebrated on Sunday in commemoration of Christ's resurrection.[27]

Early Christians also met in private homes. The family—the basic unit of society—served as a structure for Christians. Various households of faith developed and varied from city to city. The new group of believers was thus inserted into an already-existing set of relationships. As a meeting place, the house provided some degree of privacy, intimacy, and stability. Inherent in the structure was the possibility for conflict between various households in terms of power and position.[28]

While the early church experienced occasional conflicts, there was a remarkable cord of identity, unity, and strength. Various mechanisms illustrate the formation of this new identity and unity. These include the language of belonging—these believers were the "body of Christ" comprised of "brothers" and "sisters"—and the language of separation—differences existed between those who belonged to Christ and those who did not. A fine tension developed between keeping the faith and reaching out to those both in and out of the faith. The Communal Meal provided an opportunity for both physical and spiritual strength for believers. Rather than withdrawing *from* the world, the Christians carried their witness *to* the world. The early church recognized that the local body of believers was a part of the universal church comprised of all believers.[29]

Church and the Roman Empire

For numerous reasons, the Roman Empire was ready to receive the Christian message. Roman roads, law, and peace created excellent conditions for introducing the gospel to the world. The first Christians appear to have come to Rome under Emperor Claudius.[30] Christianity promised a sense of belonging to a special community with specific values in a time when local values and civic institutions were losing their potency to a distinct central government. A strict moral code with its rejection of other gods increased the Christian's sense of separateness. In addition, charitable acts increased the feeling of fellowship and communal identity.[31] Offering hope and love to all people, the message was well received. The attractiveness of the person of Christ Jesus was particularly appealing to a longing and chaotic world.[32] What had happened in Palestine would find expression in Rome and her world.

Several additional aspects of Christianity were instrumental in taking hold of the Roman world. With its acceptance in major urban areas, the Christian message established a firm foothold from which to spread. The churches were characterized by mutual cooperation and an openness to both sexes and all social classes. The Christian message contained a high degree of doctrinal unity. In addition, persecution and martyrdom, especially during the reigns of Nero and Domitian, helped to increase the strength of the Christian movement.[33]

While the New Testament, in keeping with the Jewish importance of the child, places great emphasis upon the nurture and care of the child, little is said about the child's actual training. Regarding the training of the child as a primary parental duty, the early church did not provide any kind of general education for children. Though they did not establish schools of their own, churches provided additional religious education through the family and church. Christian parents taught their children what could be accepted and what must be rejected in light of its compatibility with their Christian faith.[34]

Several possible reasons exist for this failure to establish separate Christian schools. The early church had a strong belief in the imminent second coming of Christ. Life was quickly coming to an end; therefore, it was not necessary to prepare for the future. Quite poor, the early church possessed neither buildings nor staff for such an undertaking. Days would soon come when Christianity would be illegal. Any association with the name of Christ would bring severe legal ramifications. Any one or combination of these reasons may account for the early church's failure to provide general education for its children.[35]

While the church did not formally support the education of children, parents sent their children to the current schools of the day with their Greek and Latin influence. These schools included a curriculum that focused upon the Latin poets. School organization was tied to the heathen religions. Holidays for the children were pagan religious festivals. This position is rather difficult to comprehend. Why would Christian parents send their child for instruction in pagan religions?

Tertullian, a noted Christian apologist, had a special way of viewing the situation. Adamant that no Christian should be a teacher in such a school, Tertullian nevertheless pleaded that secular education was necessary. One cannot live and study Scripture without the tools given in secular education. While the Christian teacher must teach the whole, the Christian learner (child) has the ability to know what to accept and what to reject. Other Christian leaders allowed the Christian to be a schoolteacher if it were his only way of livelihood. However, the Christian teacher must publicly announce each day his disbelief in the pagan gods.[36]

While Christians gained some protection and privilege in the Roman Empire brought about by the conversion of key government leadership, restrictions occurred periodically. In A.D. 362, Emperor Julian began instituting restrictions against Christians and their former privileges. One of the restrictions included closing the secular schools to Christian teachers. Christian students could attend, but instruction in pagan religious beliefs would be prominent. The plan may have been to deprive the church of its learned leadership and thus reduce its effectiveness in articulating its message to the world. Fortunately, the edict of Julian was rescinded by Valentinian, his successor.[37]

Catechumenal and Catechetical Schools

For those interested in joining, the early church developed catechumenal schools. The *catechumens*—people who desired to join the church—received instruction in the doctrine of the church. Taught by bishops, priests, deacons, or trained laypersons, the training period lasted from two to three years. The purpose was not for general or intellectual training; rather, it was training in church membership. The method of teaching was catechetical, or question and answer. Three levels of instruction were provided. First, there was the Hearers' class for those permitted to hear Scripture readings and sermons. Basic instruction in church doctrine was included. The second class was the Kneelers, who had been Hearers for a period of time and now had proven themselves morally worthy. When the Hearers withdrew, the Kneelers remained for prayers and advanced teaching. The third class was the Chosen who received intensive doctrinal training in preparation for baptism.[38]

Begun in the first and second centuries, catechumenal schools were highly developed between A.D. 325 and 450. After 450, the teaching deteriorated. Infant baptism was largely responsible for this decline. The church provided no teaching program for those born and baptized in the church. The clergy encouraged the home to be responsible for religious instruction. Although tremendously diminished, catechumenal teaching has continued throughout Christian history, especially in foreign mission fields.[39]

In the second and third centuries, a few locations developed highly specialized institutions known as the catechetical schools. Evolving out of catechumenal schools, catechetical schools provided a setting for the synthesis of philosophy and church doctrine. Each school was a private lectureship with an outstanding teacher. Their chief focus was theological apologetics. In order to defend Christianity from outside attack, instruction in philosophy and science was necessary.[40]

Principal catechetical schools developed in the cities of Alexandria, Caesarea, Antioch, Edessa, Nisibis, Jerusalem, and Constantinople. Noteworthy teachers and specialities were associated with these schools. For example, at Alexandria, Clement and Origen were outstanding early church teachers. At Caesarea, Eusebius, the first great church historian, wrote *Ecclesiastical History*. The Antioch center was famous for its biblical studies. The Edessa Center was later the home of the Nestorians, a group that taught a distorted view of Christ. Nisibis stressed the values of monasticism in promoting learning. The scholars at Nisibis translated the work of the Greek thinkers into Syrian, becoming agents of culture diffusion.[41]

Neither the catechumenal nor the catechetical schools replaced the ordinary elementary and secondary schools. Generally, Christian children were sent to Greek or Latin schools which were sometimes conducted by Christian teachers.[42] Soon the catechetical schools, which promoted open inquiry, gave way to schools dominated by the growing power of bishops. These schools became known as episcopal or cathedral schools. Being highly organized, they were ruled by church canon as early as the fourth century. Soon these schools came to dominate all education, and all boys destined for the priesthood attended them.

Leaders of the church had become increasingly antagonistic toward pagan learning, including the work of the Greek scholars. With the overthrow of the Roman Empire by Germanic tribesmen, Greek learning in the West was largely forgotten. These cathedral schools gradually became more and more interested in exclusively educating the priestly class. While there was intellectual aristocracy within the walls of the church, the masses remained ignorant. Learning in the coming age would occur almost exclusively within the cathedral and monastic schools. Thus, the Bible was no longer the Book of the people.[43]

Learning Activity 1.5

1. Describe the educational practices of the early church.
2. What was the early church's attitude toward secular learning?
3. What is the present-day church's attitude toward secular learning?

Monastic Movement

The Christian monastic movement developed out of the conviction that the world and the human body were corrupt. Monks had lived in the Orient centuries before the birth of Christ. They were originally hermits who withdrew from society to find a more perfect way of life. Inspired by the example of Christ, certain early Christians sought to imitate Him in a life of self-denial. Christian monasteries began in Egypt. Anthony of Egypt (A.D. 251-356) is known as the father of hermit monasticism. By going into the desert to pray and to serve, Anthony modeled the behavior that would be followed by hundreds in Egypt, Syria, and Palestine.

Communal monasteries developed in southern Egypt in the third century. Pachomius (A.D. 286-346) organized monks into a regimented life-style for the common good. Life was ordered and disciplined by a strict and growing body of rules. These little "cities of God" developed in response to nominal Christianity in a collapsing Roman world. In addition, monasticism was seen as the most perfect life of faith that could be lived, apart from martyrdom. Basil the Great (A.D. 329-379) popularized communal monasticism and expanded the monks' work into social services such as caring for the orphaned, widowed, and needy living near the communities.[44]

The leading figure in the growth of monasticism in the Western world was Benedict of Nursia (A.D. 480-547). Benedict's model of monastic life became the model for all Western monasticism. In the *Rules for Monasteries,* Benedict described a comprehensive organizational schema for the life of the order. The plan included manual labor, periods of devotion (prayer and study), and a hierarchical government directed by an abbot. His rule achieved a balance between penitential discipline and human relations within the monastic community.[45]

The abbot had the power to command obedience. Although he possessed governing power, the abbot was required to consult with all brothers before making a decision. Novices—those who wished to join the group—underwent a probationary period at the conclusion of which they took the vows of poverty, chastity, and obedience. The Benedictine Rule divided the day into seven periods that included four periods of worship and three of manual labor. Work was crucial to the monastery; monasteries became centers of industry. Two major labor activities included agriculture and the copying of precious manuscripts. The latter activity provided libraries for the world and preserved learning in an era when learning was minimal at best.[46] The personal life of the monks was characterized by regularity, consistency, and order. A variety of activities were provided, including a sensible diet and strict but merciful discipline.[47]

The monasteries did not all remain small. While they varied in size, larger monasteries included hospitals, travelers' quarters, quarters for the poor, kitchens and refectories, dormitories, farm buildings, shops, and a church. Because boys were often dedicated to the monastic life at age seven, schools were a necessity. Two types of students were admitted to monastery schools. The first were the *oblati,* those intended for the monastic life; the second were the *externi,* those students who paid fees. Often these groups of students were divided into separate schools.[48]

Monastic schools involved a usually strict and somber approach to learning. The course of study focused upon Latin and the seven liberal arts, composed of the trivium and quadrivium. The young scholars had to learn to speak Latin, and for most of the students, the learning of Latin was a new experience. Training was not given in their own vernacular language. The students began by studying the trivium, comprised of grammar, rhetoric, and logic. Grammar involved the study of various works in Latin. Rhetoric involved various aspects of composition such as letter writing, record keeping, and preparing of legal documents. Logic involved the study of the works of Aristotle.

After studying the trivium, the more gifted students progressed to the study of the quadrivium, comprised of arithmetic, geometry, astronomy, and music. The trivium and quadrivium formed the basic pattern for study throughout Europe. The seven liberal arts were studied not for themselves but in preparation for the study of theology, the greatest discipline of all. Monastic education was essentially religious education.[49] From the seventh to the thirteenth century, there was practically no other education available except that offered by monks.[50]

One of the most significant aspects in educational history from the seventh to the thirteenth centuries was the educational work and reform of Emperor Charlemagne (742-814), or Charles the Great, of France. In a world that was characteristically ignorant, Charlemagne proposed significant educational and religious reforms. In 782 Charlemagne turned his palace into a school and requested teachers from various parts of Europe to assist him. The most famous teacher was Alcuin (735-804) of the cathedral school at York, England.

Through Charlemagne's influence, the Council of Aachen (789) decreed that convents and cathedrals must establish schools for the education of boys. Priests were required to pass literary examinations. Charlemagne imported gifted teachers from Rome for his schools. Monastery schools were opened to those students not intended for monastic life. Priests were ordered to maintain schools for all who came to them for instruction. Instruction was to be given without charge. No one was to be baptized who could not repeat the Apostles' Creed and the Lord's Prayer. Charlemagne encouraged the church to assume its responsibility of education for both clergy and laity. In spite of these sweeping reforms, after Charlemagne's death the empire crumbled, and his educational reforms diminished. Another significant individual who shared Charlemagne's vision was Alfred the Great (849-901), king of England. Alfred encouraged the education of the clergy and the use of the vernacular language.[51]

High Middle Ages

In the High Middle Ages (1000-1300), significant changes occurred that would enhance the spread and reform of education. Various institutions emerged that included "national" monarchies in France, England, and Germany. In addition, the European borders were relatively secure from foreign invasions. An increased food supply and a growing population developed. Increased trade and commerce brought the emergence of a merchant class. Most significantly, the recovery of ancient Greek manuscripts created a renewed interest in education.[52]

Apart from selected education of the clergy, formal education for the majority of the population of Europe had stopped in the early Middle Ages. Although the congregations were illiterate, certain educational practices continued. Symbolic teaching occurred through religious drama and the use of the sacraments. Because large numbers of people had been brought into the church without benefit of instruction, actual Christian belief and practice had become intertwined with pagan beliefs and superstitions.

Crusades.—One of the most significant series of events that lead to the renewed interest in learning and the subsequent Protestant Reformation was the Crusades. The Crusades were an attempt by the Roman Catholic Church to regain control of Jerusalem and the Holy Lands from the Moslem invaders. In the medieval church, pilgrimages were a way of obtaining forgiveness for post-baptismal sins. A pilgrimage to Jerusalem was a high achievement. Though the Muhammadans had captured Jerusalem in the seventh century, they nevertheless allowed Christian pilgrims to visit Jerusalem. However, the Seljuk Turks captured the Holy Lands in the eleventh century, and they were not sympathetic to Christian pilgrims.

In 1095 Pope Urban II called upon secular authorities to devote themselves to a divine crusade to recapture the Holy Lands. Having been promised forgiveness of sins if they died in the effort, approximately 500,000 soldiers began the move toward the east. Approximately 40,000 reached Jerusalem and recaptured it. Eight other crusades followed and ended in a children's crusade in 1212.

The Crusades had various impacts upon the European world. The papacy was strengthened not only in power and influence but in wealth. The Crusades opened European eyes to a new world of trade, ideas, and literature. Ancient manuscripts were rediscovered. Commerce and trade were fostered, and a new middle class arose. While the Middle Ages were noted for a lack of education and belief in superstition, the Crusades strengthened the already-existing superstitions, especially regarding relics. The Crusades contributed both directly and indirectly to the educational changes and reforms that followed.[53]

Universities.—The twelfth and thirteenth centuries witnessed the development of universities, largely out of the cathedral schools. The first important Western university was in Bologna, Italy. Here the first formal organization of students and professors and the granting of degrees occurred. This university, like the others to come, was organized along the lines of the trade guilds. Originally a union of professors and students, the university was organized for self-interest and mutual protection from townspeople. The "university" was a program of study that afforded the student a license to teach others.

These early universities moved from one location to another, dependent upon the resources and support of the community. Concern was on scholarship, not buildings. Eventually, universities became legally incorporated entities, and a degree of self-government arose with specific rights for both professors and students.[54]

Various universities emerged, each with its own specialization based upon the interests, gifts, and resources of the university and the surrounding community. Early universities included the University of Naples, which specialized in medicine; the University of Paris, which specialized in theology; and the University of Bologna, which specialized in law. Later universities included Rome, Oxford, and Cambridge. The Cambridge University model would be followed in the American colonies with the founding of Harvard College. In keeping with the traditions of the cathedral and monastic schools, the universities emphasized the trivium and the quadrivium. With the discovery of ancient manuscripts, learning began to include complete works of Aristotle, Ptolemy, Euclid, and other Latin classics. The chief educational methodology within the university system became known as Scholasticism.[55]

Scholastic Movement.—The Scholastic movement rose to prominence from 1000 to 1300 within the medieval schools. Scholastics sought to support church doctrine through rational argument. In the Middle Ages, the Church controlled "truth," but the world slowly began to ask questions. Scholasticism attempted to reconcile faith and reason. Generally, Scholasticism regarded faith and reason as complementary sources of truth. Scholastics accepted Scripture as the revealed Word of God. Reasoning deductively and syllogistically from these prior principles found in God's Word, humanity could discover God's universal truth. Two leading Scholastics were Peter Abelard (1079-1142) and Thomas Aquinas (1225-1274).

In the university setting, the learning process was rather basic. Because of a scarcity of books, most teaching took the form of lectures. The students composed commentaries on authoritative texts, especially Aristotle. Striving for independent and undiscovered truth was not encouraged. Rather, the student was to organize and harmonize already established truth. In the scholastic method, the learner read traditional authorities, summarized the research, composed arguments both pro and con, and then drew a conclusion. Emphasis was not upon original, creative thought but proving what was already known or accepted.[56]

Brethren of the Common Life.—One of the most influential of the religious and educational pre-Reformation groups was the Brethren of the Common Life. Gerhard Groote (1340-1384), a native of the Netherlands and graduate of the University of Paris, took the message of reform to the people in the cities of the lower Rhine. Groote called all individuals—clergy and laypersons—to a new devotion. Known as the Brethren of the Common Life, these individuals lived in communities called "houses." These houses involved all levels of society. Their goal was to recreate primitive Christianity as they lived and worked in the outside world. The Brethren translated large portions of Scripture into their mother tongue and distributed literature to the people. Preaching in the vernacular instead of Latin the Brethren called for practical Christian living and denounced the Roman Church.[57]

One of the most significant contributions of the Brethren was the revitalization of Christian education. One of the Brethren to become a teacher was John Cele. Prior to Cele's day, religious training consisted of learning the Lord's Prayer, the Ten Commandments, and the Apostles' Creed. Cele introduced the idea of teaching the Bible on all days of the week, not just on Sunday, so individuals could acquire the ability and the right to read Scriptures for themselves.[58]

Wycliffe.—John Wycliffe (1320-1384) led a second pre-Reformation group interested in biblical instruction. Like the Brethren, Wycliffe was shocked at the immorality of the Roman Catholic Church and the low spiritual life of her members. Wycliffe asserted that supreme power lay not in the Pope or the church hierarchy but in Scripture itself. He preached to the masses and began a translation of the Vulgate (Latin Bible) into English.[59] Wycliffe's followers became known as Lollards, and they went out two-by-two, preaching and teaching. For their rebellion against Church authority, significant numbers of Lollards were burned at the stake. Because of persecution for preaching and teaching direct access to Scripture and God, the Lollards went underground after 1431.[60]

Learning Activity 1.6

1. What contributions did monasticism make to Christian education?
2. Describe positive benefits of the Crusades to medieval Europe.
3. Describe Scholasticism. What are its strengths and weaknesses? Does Scholasticism exist today?
4. Are there any modern-day equivalents to the Brethren of the Common life? Explain.

Notes

1. E. D. Hirsch, *Cultural Literacy: What Every American Needs to Know* (Boston: Houghton Mifflin Co., 1987), 2.
2. C. B. Eavey, *History Of Christian Education* (Chicago: Moody Press, 1964), 51.
3. William Barclay, *Educational Ideals in the Ancient World* (Grand Rapids: Baker Book House, 1959), 14-16.
4. Eavey, 54-56.
5. Ibid., 56-57.
6. Ibid., 59-62.
7. H. I. Hester, *The Heart of Hebrew History: A Study of the Old Testament* (Liberty, Mo.: Quality Press, 1962), 256-57.
8. Robert H. Gundry, *A Survey of the New Testament* (Grand Rapids: Zondervan Press, 1970), 41-42.
9. H. G. Good, *A History of Western Education*, 2d ed. (New York: Macmillan Company, 1960), 14.
10. Barclay, 42.
11. Michael Grant, *The History of Ancient Israel* (New York: Charles Scribner's Sons, 1984), 216-19.
12. Ibid.
13. Eavey, 65.
14. Barclay, 44.
15. Grant, 217-18.
16. Gundry, 49-51.
17. Eavey, 67.
18. Hayyim Schauss, *The Jewish Festivals: History and Observance,* trans. Samuel Jaffe (New York: Schocken Books, 1938), 13-16.
19. J. M. Price, *Jesus the Teacher* (Nashville: Convention Press, 1946), 5-6.

20. Ibid., 6.

21. Eavey, 78-79.

22. Ibid., 79.

23. Frederick Mayer, *A History of Educational Thought*, 2d ed. (Columbus, Ohio: Charles E. Merrill Books, Inc., 1966), 127.

24. Lewis J. Sherrill, *The Rise of Christian Education* (New York: Macmillan Co., 1944), 144-51.

25. Charles A. Tidwell, *Educational Ministry of a Church* (Nashville: Broadman Press, 1982), 39.

26. Donald M. Lake, "Baptism," *The New International Dictionary of the Christian Church*, rev. ed., gen. ed. J. D. Douglas (Grand Rapids: Zondervan Press, 1978), 99-101.

27. H. L. Ellison, "Sunday," *The New International Dictionary of the Christian Church*, rev. ed., gen. ed. J. D. Douglas (Grand Rapids: Zondervan Press, 1978), 939-40.

28. Wayne A. Meeks, *The First Urban Christians: The Social World of the Apostle Paul* (New Haven, Conn.: Yale University Press, 1983), 74-76.

29. Ibid., 84-107.

30. L. P. Wilkinson, *The Roman Experience* (New York: Alfred D. Knopf, 1974), 195.

31. Fritiz M. Heichelheim, Cedric A. Yes, and Alfred M. Ward. *A History of the Roman People*, 2d ed. (Englewood Cliffs, N.J.: Prentice-Hall Co., 1984), 390-92.

32. Wilkinson, 196.

33. Heichelheim, Yes, and Ward, 390-92.

34. Wilkinson, 200-1

35. Barclay, 238-39.

36. Ibid., 238-40.

37. Ibid., 243-50.

38. Eavey, 85-86.

39. Ibid., 86-88.

40. Ibid., 87-88.

41. Good, 62-63.

42. Ibid., 63.

43. Eavey, 88-90.

44. Donald Kagan, Steven Ozment, and Frank M. Turner, *The Western Heritage*, 2d ed. (New York: Macmillan Publishing Co., 1983), 258-59.

45. Edward Peters, *Europe and the Middle Ages* (Englewood Cliffs, N.J.: Prentice-Hall, 1983), 48.

46. Good, 67.

47. Peters, 48.

48. Good, 69.

49. Ibid., 70-73.

50. Paul Monroe, *A Text-Book in the History of Education* (New York: Macmillan Co., 1905), 253.

51. Good, 73-76.

52. Kagan, Ozment, and Turner, 283-84.

53. Robert A. Baker, *A Summary of Christian History* (Nashville: Broadman Press, 1959), 121-24.

54. Kagan, Ozment, and Turner, 299-300.

55. Good, 102-3, and Mayer, 156-57.

56. Kagan, Ozment, and Turner, 301.

57. Frederick Eby, *The Development of Modern Education: In Theory, Organization and Practice,* 2d ed. (Englewood Cliffs, N.J.: Prentice-Hall, 1952), 13-15.

58. Ibid., 23-25.

59. Ibid., 15-16.

60. Baker, *A Summary of Christian History,* 160-61.

2
Historical Background for Christian Education: Renaissance to the Present

An Overview of the Relationship Theme

The Renaissance signified humanity's transition from the medieval to the modern world. Two renaissances existed—the Italian, or Southern, Renaissance and the Northern Renaissance. The Italian Renaissance provided an education for an elite few in the Greek and Latin classics. The Northern Renaissance sought to provide an education for all in biblical and classical studies.

The Northern Renaissance laid fertile ground for the Protestant Reformation. The Reformation, led by Martin Luther, John Calvin, and John Knox, sought to bring an education to all people. The Bible was translated into various languages, and the invention of the printing press aided in making it more accessible. People were encouraged to read the Bible and to experience personal salvation. Not focusing only upon the future life, the Reformation stressed responsible living and taught that people have a responsibility in their relationships with others.

The Roman Catholic Church sought to counteract the effects of Protestant education across Europe. Catholic reactions included the Jesuits, who sought to indoctrinate the young men into Catholic ideology; the Port Royalists, who used all educational resources available to help redeem souls; and the Brethren of Christian Schools, who sought to provide a common elementary school system for the poor.

In the New World, the religious practices of the colonists reflected their homeland. In North America, the history of American education is chiefly that of Christian education. Stressing the importance of salvation and Scripture, the early Protestant settlers emphasized education. Schools were established which would educate not only on an elementary level but also on a university level. Christian colleges sought to provide the needed colonial leadership.

With westward expansion came the need to provide Bibles and other Christian literature for those on the frontier. Those responding to such a need founded the American Bible Society and the American Sunday School Union. In spite of the general indifference of churches, the Sunday School Union promoted the establishment of Sunday Schools across the country. Sunday Schools in America became a place where all could jointly study God's Word. The Union often provided both a general education and libraries for many sections of the country. Gradually, Sunday Schools were accepted by churches and became aligned with various denominations.

The Common School movement emerged and sought to promote a public education system based upon common elements of Christian morality. Gradually, churches became less involved in private education and concentrated more attention upon the Sunday School. However, elements of liberal theology weakened many churches in Sunday School growth. Other evangelical groups have, however, experienced widespread growth of their Sunday Schools.

One denomination in particular, Southern Baptists, began to emphasize the Sunday School as a method of Bible study and church outreach. Through concerted efforts of organization, worker training, and literature publication, the Sunday School aided the growth of Southern Baptist churches across the United States. Increased biblical study paralleled church growth and development.

Christian education has become a vast enterprise. Denominations devote much effort to Christian literature publication and promotion. Christian education can be found beginning with the preschool level and extending to the graduate level. Christian television programming has become a large-scale operation. Christian education possesses great opportunity and responsibility. Whatever the facet, Christian education continues to be responsible for making the Word of God available to all. Consistent with its beginnings, true Christian education seeks to help individuals align themselves relationally with God's Word in both blessings and demands.

Renaissance and Reformation

Southern or Italian Renaissance

Often the Renaissance is described as the transitional period from the medieval world to the modern world. Difficulty exists in pinpointing a specific birth date for the Renaissance. The Renaissance actually consists of two different renaissances, each with its own distinctive qualities. The first is the Southern, or Italian, Renaissance whose dates are approximately 1300 to 1600. Italy's trade contact with other countries and her possession of Greek and Latin manuscripts influenced this Renaissance's beginning in southern Italy.[1]

Two pivotal leaders of the Southern Renaissance were Petrarch (1304-74) and Boccaccio (1313-75). Rejecting Aristotelian Scholasticism, these leaders and others turned to Cicero, Quintilian, and to secular dimensions of experience. Humanism (interest in the humanities—anything pertaining to mankind) describes their movement, with its recovery of classical thought and application to contemporary human dilemmas. The Renaissance scholar wanted to understand each classical writing in itself and its historical setting. Prior to this renewed interest, text and commentary were often intertwined in such a fashion that it was difficult to differentiate between the two. Rediscovered Latin and Greek manuscripts helped solve this problem. Rather than reading and confusing commentary with text, the Renaissance scholar sought to edit commentary from the actual ancient text.[2]

The Southern Renaissance represented individual humanism with its focus upon personal culture, individual freedom, and development. The resulting humanistic education provided the basis for modern academic freedom with its central tenets of freedom of thought, self-expression, and creative pursuits. Essentially, the best of the Greek liberal education that incorporated a holistic view of man, the development of the mind, body, and morals in harmony was sought.[3]

The fullest possible enjoyment of life was sought for the individual. Only the educated person could appreciate the past and enjoy the present to the fullest capacity. Because textbooks became more available, formal lectures were less necessary. Written themes replaced oral debates. While advances in scholarship were achieved in the Southern Renaissance, scholarship was limited to an elite group. The great majority of people were untouched by the advances in the Southern Renaissance.[4]

Northern Renaissance

Various conditions promoted the growth and development of the Renaissance north of the Alps. These conditions included the Brethren of the Common Life, the traveling of French scholars of Italy, the invention of movable printing type developed by Gutenberg, the fall of Constantinople with its scholars fleeing westward, and the discoveries by the Dutch and English explorers.[5]

The Northern Renaissance (1450-1600) differed significantly from its southern counterpart. Unlike the Southern Renaissance, with its focus upon the individual life's pleasures, the Northern Renaissance focused upon practical religious and social concerns of the masses. A rich and full life was sought for all members of society.[6] Desiderius Erasmus (1466-1536), one of the leading figures in the movement, believed the free exchange of ideas was necessary for intellectual growth and development. He believed that men are primarily brothers who share a common home. Education can promote brotherly understanding and conduct. Highly forceful and hopeful in education, Erasmus claimed that the hope of the state was in the education of its youth. Both governments and individuals could be enlightened through education.[7]

The northern humanists stressed religious, moral, and social education much more than their southern counterparts. Religious instruction was blended with liberal classical training. In the north, an attempt was made for more democratic education. Secondary and higher education received primary emphasis, and the curriculum included both biblical and classical literature.[8]

Reformation

Pinpointing the exact date or beginning of the Protestant Reformation is difficult. The most commonly accepted date is October 31, 1517, when Martin Luther posted his "Ninety-Five Theses" on the door of the Castle Church in Wittenberg, Germany. These statements called for debate with the Church on issues such as the sale of indulgences, the power of the Pope in forgiving guilt, and the church's treasury of merits donated by Christ and the saints.[9] A forceful challenge was issued, and a break began in the Christian world.

Other factors contributed to the Reformation. Previous attempts had been made at reforming aspects of the church, including the reforms brought about by the Renaissance, the growing political authority of local rulers, and general dismay with the corrupt practices of many in the Church.

Though volumes have been written on the Reformation, the focus here is on the change in education. Efforts begun in the Northern Renaissance found fulfillment in the Reformation with a revolution in various aspects of Christian education. With the Protestant emphasis on the Bible, a new need and opportunity to read emerged.[10] Developed by Johann Gutenberg around 1445, the printing press with its movable type made possible the mass production of Bibles.[11] In addition, the Bible needed to be translated into common languages for all people. Humanistic studies included Hebrew and Greek so that classics could be read in the original languages. This language emphasis appealed to Protestant reformers, and by the end of the sixteenth century, various religious and educational changes had resulted.[12]

The Reformation challenged the beliefs, practices, and privileges of the Roman Catholic Church. In some locations, the Reformation eliminated, minimized, or placed restrictions on:

mandatory fasting; auricular confession; the veneration of the saints, relics, and images; indulgences; pilgrimages and shrines; vigils; weekly, monthly, and annual Masses for the dead; the belief in purgatory; Latin worship services; the sacrifice of the Mass; numerous religious ceremonies, festivals, and holidays; the canonical hours; monasteries and mendicant orders; the sacramental status of marriage, extreme unction, confirmation, holy orders, and penance; clerical celibacy; clerical immunity from civil taxation and criminal jurisdiction; nonresident benefices; excommunication and interdict; canon law; episcopal and papal authority; and the traditional Scholastic education of the clergy.[13]

Prior to discussing specific contributions of selected reformers, general summary statements will be made regarding Protestant education. Throughout history, the Catholic Church had been the guardian of teaching. Similarly Protestant churches regarded teaching as one of their most important functions. Protestant churches advocated that everyone—male and female—should be instructed in the Scriptures. Such a scriptural knowledge would be the basis for faith and life.[14] In countries with Protestant rulers, control of the schools was transferred to the state, state school systems were established, and universal education was promoted.[15] This education would be based upon Scripture, doctrinal creeds, and other religious materials.

The overall educational objective was the preparation of individuals who would lead worthy lives on earth. This emphasis was similar to that of Hebrew education. Consequently, preparation for the duties of home, occupation, church, and state were stressed. With the Bible as the primary text, schools typically employed formal methods of instruction. Great attention was given to the memorization of catechisms, grammar rules, and larger passages from the classics. Often these schools shared the same type of strict formalism as earlier Catholic schools. Rather than teaching them how to think, the schools often instructed the children in what to think.[16]

Martin Luther (1483-1546).—The leading figure in the Reformation, Luther gave particular emphasis to the role of education. Although highly critical of each other, both Luther and Erasmus are credited with establishing the foundations of Bible study and devotion that proved to be central tenets of the Reformation.[17] Luther advocated public compulsory education that included religious instruction as well as trade and vocational training. He proposed that civil authorities support and control elementary schools.

While all individuals should receive religious training, only the most capable should go to Latin schools. These individuals would become the leaders in law, civil service, medicine, and especially theology. Education as a whole was the threefold responsibility of the school, church, and home. Passionately believing in this idea of responsibility, Luther argued that individuals should not marry and have children until they were able to teach the children.[18]

Interested in higher education, Luther led the reform of the arts curriculum at the University of Wittenberg. Although Luther believed that the humanities were an excellent example of human creative capacities, he also acknowledged that the humanities were fruitless in terms of redemption. Luther encouraged the humanistic disciplines such as rhetoric, languages, and history in opposition to the dialectical and scholastic debates. Assisted by Philip Melanchthon (1497-1560), Luther worked for religious and educational reform that would bring new light and life to a growing Protestant Europe.[19]

John Calvin (1509-1564).—Another leading reformer, John Calvin, had tremendous influence in the newly-developing Protestant educational system. Like Luther, Calvin proposed a dual-track system of education. Common people would be educated in vernacular schools with emphasis upon catechisms, religious material, reading, writing, history, and arithmetic. Upper-class children pursuing higher education would attend classical Latin grammar schools. These schools would prepare future ministers, lawyers, and educators by emphasizing the classical studies of Latin, Greek, and Hebrew for higher education.[20] The state should legislate laws for the support and functioning of schools based upon church recommendations.

Through incorporating several struggling Latin schools, Calvin established the Academy of Geneva in 1559. While the school was under supervision of the city, it was supported by tuition fees. The school gave primary emphasis to religious training. Classes began with morning prayers and ended with the repeating of the Lord's Prayer and the offering of thanks. From eleven to twelve o'clock, the student engaged in singing psalms. At four in the afternoon, focus was given to reciting the Lord's Prayer, the confession of faith, and the Ten Commandments. Students and faculty listened to a sermon on Wednesday mornings. On Saturday afternoons, the students studied the catechism. Sundays were devoted to religious worship services and meditating on the sermon.

The school became a model for the organization of the Universities of Leyden in Holland and Edinburgh in Scotland and Emmanuel College at Cambridge University. Graduates of Cambridge conveyed Calvin's influence to colonial New England. Calvinistic faith created a high enthusiasm for education.[21] A significant number of Calvin's pupils were foreigners. Having completed their study, these highly trained Calvinists returned to their native lands and promoted new models of Calvinistic education.[22]

In addition to focusing upon formal schooling, Calvin emphasized the importance of family education. Parents were expected to teach their children the catechism and Christian living. Every home was visited once a year to determine that church regulations were being carried out.[23] Considering children as conceived and born in sin, education sought to instill discipline and thereby cure the child's inclination to sin. Rejecting play as idleness, Calvinist education justified corporal punishment.[24]

John Knox (1505-1572).—In Scotland, John Knox introduced Calvin's Geneva model of education.[25] In *First Book of Discipline*, Knox proposed a self-governing church similar to the one in Geneva. Responsible for the control of morals and religion, the church should control public and private education. Knox envisioned a comprehensive hierarchy of education. Each church should sponsor an elementary school, each town should sponsor a secondary school, and each city should sponsor a university. The wealth of the monasteries and churches and all tithes should be devoted to the support of the churches, the schools, and the poor.[26]

Post-Reformation Educational Reactions

Prior to the Protestant Reformation, the Roman Church had begun to put into effect various measures designed to control growing independence and deviation from traditional beliefs and practices. Attempts included checks on clergy licentiousness and church abuse, the index of forbidden books, strengthening the education of priests, the Council of Trent, and the founding of the Jesuit Order.[27]

Jesuits.—The Society of Jesus, more commonly known as the Jesuits, was founded by Ignatius Loyola (1491-1556). It created a new educational system to combat the Reformation. Formerly a soldier, Loyola chose to devote himself as a spiritual crusader for the church. The Jesuits' goals included combating heresy, advancing the interests of the church, and strengthening the authority of the papacy.[28]

The contributions of the Jesuits found expression largely through their educational efforts.[29] The spirit of the Renaissance had focused upon the importance of individualism. Regarding individualism as dangerous, the Jesuits held that such belief was in conflict with the obedience and submission required to Christ and His Church. The Jesuits sought to produce individuals who conformed to the kingdom of God as demonstrated by the Roman Catholic Church. The Jesuits sought to produce individuals proficient in the seven liberal arts and selected classical Latin authors.

With respect to the learning processes, Jesuits held that the young male learner must be separated from all outside influences. Indoctrination was the method to achieve control of human personality. Relying on the scholastic method, the Jesuits gave attention to drill, repetition, memorization, and strict discipline.[30] The Jesuits fostered learning by stimulating interest and competition, rather than learning by flogging.[31]

Jesuits were not interested in training the masses but in teaching the church leaders who would control the masses.[32] The Society assumed responsibility for training vast numbers of teachers and for assisting the spread of the Catholic Church in the New World, and their educational reputation grew. Wealthy fathers often requested their sons, even those with no priestly intents, receive a Jesuit education. Numerous schools and colleges developed, particularly in Germany.[33] Additionally, the Jesuits had powerful influence over future rulers through their educational endeavors.[34] Because of the aggressive nature of the order, the Jesuits soon came into conflict with civil authorities. Various charges were made against the order. The order was suppressed by Pope Clement XIV in 1773 and later revived in 1814.

Port Royalists.—The Port Royalists reacted against the work and methods of the Jesuits. Du Vergier de Hauranne, or Saint Cyran, a key leader in the movement, encouraged the formation of the schools of Port Royal in 1646. These schools were Latin schools for the training of church and state leadership. Although they would exist less than twenty years, these schools, located near Port Royal, France, had tremendous significance in the teaching of language and logic.

The aim of this teaching group emerged from the Augustinian doctrine of total human depravity from conception. The goal was the transformation of corrupt human nature into one of purity and holiness. Higher education sought to develop individuals who would utilize all resources, such as science, literature, and eloquence, in the redeeming of souls. To be useful to God's service, the individual must be able to speak, to think, and to act. Books and other materials were selected which would stimulate the student to use judgment and reflection. Curriculum materials must have impact upon the religious life and must be comprehensible by the child through the senses. Port Royalist methods included: use of the vernacular (French) rather than Latin, emphasis upon phonetics, and an emphasis on memorization only after understanding. This teaching order stressed a strict and personal devotion to God as much as did the Calvinists. Pressured by Jesuit influence, the Pope disbanded the Port Royalists in 1661.[35]

Brethren of Christian Schools.—The Brethren of Christian Schools established by Jean Baptiste de La Salle (1651-1719) in 1684 was one of the most influential of the teaching orders established for elementary education. This attempt was the first one by the Catholic Church to establish a common school system. Originally, the brothers were not priests, but after 1694, the brothers took the priestly vows. Their goal was to provide a free elementary and religious education in the vernacular of the poor. Brethren methods included grouping children by ability; emphasizing reading, writing, and spelling skills; and administering mildly prescribed discipline.[36]

Learning Activity 2.1

1. Apart from geographical locations, what are the differences between the Italian Renaissance and the Northern Renaissance?
2. What is the relationship between the Renaissance and the Reformation?
3. Are there any evidences today that current educational practices have their origins in Reformation ideals? Explain.

The Church in America

While additional educational changes would continue in Europe, a basic thesis of this discussion has been demonstrated. In the Protestant Reformation, the Bible had reached the hands of laypersons. Educational practices would gradually attempt to prepare men and women to read and, in some cases, to think critically about what was being read. The fruits of the Reformation would continue in the New World. The major focus of this summary will be upon the Protestant influences carried on by the early English colonists. Only briefly will Spanish influences, representing Roman Catholicism, be discussed.

Spanish Influences

Christian education occurred early among Spanish colonies of the New World. Numerous Catholic orders began the task of teaching the Spanish language, Christian religion, and various aspects of European civilization to the native Americans. Music was essential for religious services, so the teaching of music became a priority. In 1553, the University of Mexico was founded. Later developments of the Spanish colonies resulted in the establishment of a mission system which included the establishment of towns with parish churches and schools.[37]

English Influences

Largely, the history of education in colonial America is the history of Christian education. The two were closely intertwined, as the early English settlers were mostly Protestants who felt that the gospel was the means to personal salvation. In order to be saved one needed to know Scripture; to know Scripture one needed to be able to read. Many Christians left the Old World for religious freedom in the New World. The pattern of education varied with the settler and his geographical location in the Old World.

The New England colonies closely followed the educational patterns of old England. Since the early settlers came to perpetuate their faith, attention was centered around establishing schools. In addition, Puritan education, strongly influenced by Calvinism, began with strict family-centered teachings. Puritan families followed the apprenticeship system. Children learned vocational skills from older skilled workmen. Early laws reflected this concern for education. In 1635 the people of Boston voted in a town meeting to request a schoolmaster for their children. A 1647 law stated that every town with fifty householders must employ a teacher. The teacher must be paid a fixed salary. Every town of one hundred householders must provide a grammar school to prepare youth for college.[38]

The primary instructional material was called a "hornbook." The hornbook was a piece of wood with a wooden handle. A sheet of paper with the lesson printed on it was attached to the wood and covered with transparent horn. This hornbook consisted of the alphabet in upper and lower case, the Lord's Prayer, and the apostolic benediction. The hornbook was used primarily in the lower grades. After mastering the hornbook, the child was ready for the catechism, which instructed groups in basic religious beliefs. One of the most widely used catechisms was the "Westminster Catechism." After the catechism, the child was ready for studying the Bible, if opportunity allowed.

Introduced in 1690, the *New England Primer* became the adopted model in all of the colonies except Virginia, in which Anglicanism was the established religion. This work replaced the hornbook and the "Westminster Catechism." The text was used until the early part of the nineteenth century. Full of moral teachings, the *New England Primer* could be found in every home and book store, with an estimated three million copies published and sold.[39]

The leaders in the New England colonies quickly realized that the supply of individuals needed for public affairs was not keeping pace with the expanding colonial needs. While wealthy colonists in Virginia were able to send their children to England for training, this plan was not feasible to meet the growing demands in New England. Colleges would be required for the training of pastors, teachers, and other public servants.

In order to go to college, the student had to meet basic entrance requirements. Grammar school was required to obtain knowledge of the Latin language. In 1636 Harvard College was founded for the preparation of ministers. Harvard was based upon the model established at Cambridge University. Other colleges would soon follow. In time, issues of doctrinal purity came into question. In 1701, because of the feeling that the faith was being weakened at Harvard, conservative theologians led in the establishment of a new college, Yale College. To safeguard this institution, the governing body consisted of eleven clergymen.[40]

In both origin and character, these early colleges were distinctly English. This observation is no surprise considering that these early colleges were required to undergo close examination by British officials prior to granting the needed charter. Most of the teachers and organizers of these early American colleges and universities were drawn from Cambridge and Oxford. Other similarities existed in the American and the British colleges in terms of entrance requirements, forms of government, religious discipline, prescription of study, and degree requirements. College study consisted of the seven liberal arts, Renaissance languages, and Calvinistic religious training. The system itself was an apprenticeship into the practice of Renaissance life.[41]

Learning Activity 2.2

1. What was the role of education in the New England colonies?
2. Trace the origins of the Puritan religious education displayed in the New World.
3. What was the original purpose of colleges and universities established in the New World?
4. Examine the original stated purpose of your school. You may find this statement in your college catalog. Does the overall curriculum support this original purpose? Explain.

Modern Sunday School Movement

In an excellent work, *The Big Little School House*, Robert Lynn and Elliott Wright give an interesting and informative account of the Sunday School movement that has shaped American and Protestant Christianity for over two hundred years. The origins of the Sunday School are often vague and controversial, depending upon definition and historian. The modern Sunday School Movement began in 1780 with Robert Raikes in Sooty Alley, England. The Industrial Age forced large numbers of children into factories for long work hours during the week. Working long hours and having no time or interest in education, these young children roamed the streets on Sundays. Out of concern for the welfare of these children, interested individuals began establishing classes for their instruction on Sunday. William Fox, a devout Baptist, and others established in 1785 the Sunday School Society for organizing, encouraging, and supporting Sunday Schools throughout England. By the time of Raikes' death in 1811, Sunday Schools were widely established in England.[42]

Various groups dedicated to educating the poor emerged. The Society for Promoting Christian Knowledge and similar organizations secured finances for the education of children. Despite these efforts, however, two barriers remained in teaching so many children: limited financial resources and limited available teachers. The Reverend Andrew Bell and, later, Joseph Lancaster independently conceived the system of monitorial instruction. In the plan, the headmaster taught the lesson to the more mature and intelligent males. These boys then taught smaller groups of males. Thus, one head teacher could teach many hundreds of children. This system achieved great popularity in England, North America, and South America. While this method dealt with the expense issue, questions remained regarding the effectiveness of the newly-trained student-teachers.[43]

In the United States, Sunday School played a significant role in the development of basic American attitudes and institutions. While the Sunday School movement in England was targeted at the poor, in America the movement became more enlarged. Lyman Beecher (1775-1863), father of Henry Ward Beecher and Harriet Beecher Stowe, prevented the movement from becoming exclusively aimed at the poor. Rather than focusing on bringing children of the poor to the Sunday School, Beecher sought to have the children of the best families in Sunday School. The movement became one that would attract all classes. Sunday School provided an opportunity for all individuals to socialize. This concept became an illustration of one aspect of the middle-class American ideal.[44]

Rather than embracing the Sunday School movement, the early churches of America were skeptical about the use of a school connected with Sunday. In fact, many ministers considered it sinful to engage in such study on the Lord's Day. The indifference of pastors to the work of the Sunday School contributed to its lack of support in its early years.[45] Acceptance was much more varied in the South. Attitudes against education of blacks were intensified with Nat Turner's slave rebellion in 1831 in which a number of white persons were killed. Turner had received his education in Sunday School. By 1835 all Southern states had legislation against the education of slaves. The Sunday School Movement often was associated with Black education.[46]

As in England, the Sunday School was not a part of local churches. Rather, Sunday Schools were conducted by interested individuals or groups.[47] By 1790 these nondenominational schools, staffed by paid teachers, were organized in several states. The early growth of the movement was hindered by the isolated location of the churches, poor transportation, and inadequate buildings. However, the Sunday School Movement would reach the churches through the work of those fervently committed to providing biblical instruction.[48]

From 1785 to 1815, a number of Sunday Schools based on the English voluntary model were founded in Virginia. In 1785 William Elliot set aside each Sunday evening for instructing his own children as well as the servants and slaves working on his plantation. For the next forty years, the modern Sunday School Movement was largely independent of the church. After 1810, churches began to allow Sunday Schools to be held in their buildings without requiring them to pay rent. When the churches began to offer such support, the movement began to be strongly influenced by denominational or sectarian viewpoints.[49]

The Sunday School movement became particularly significant in the westward expansion of the growing United States.[50] Organizations in the east were established to print and distribute Christian literature for the frontier regions of the United States that lacked Bibles and other religious literature. Samuel J. Mills made two tours of the frontier boundaries of the United States in 1812-13 and 1814-15. At Kaskaskia, then capital of Illinois, Mills found five Bibles among the one hundred families. Such conditions led to the foundation of the American Bible Society in New York in 1816.[51] Between 1829 and 1930, this national organization made a systematic campaign to place Bibles in every home in the country. In addition, entering foreign immigrants were to be supplied with Bibles as they entered the ports of the United States.[52]

Learning Activity 2.3

1. What was the intent and audience of the first Sunday Schools?
2. What significance did Lancaster have to the Sunday School Movement? Is there any biblical basis for the Lancaster method? Why or why not?
3. Describe the environment in which the early Sunday School Movement developed in the United States. What are the current attitudes and environment toward the Sunday School?
4. What is the relationship between the Sunday School Movement and the westward expansion of the United States?
5. Examine the history of the Sunday School in your own local church. Discuss with your minister the possibility of celebrating the role of the Sunday School in your church.

Interest in Sunday Schools continued to grow across the young nation. In 1824 the American Sunday School Union was formed by clerical and lay delegates from fifteen or more of the existing twenty-four states.[53] Its constitution read: "To concentrate the efforts of Sabbath-School Societies in the different sections of our country; to strengthen the hands of the friends of religious instruction on the Lord's Day; to disseminate useful information, circulate moral and religious publications in every part of the land, and to endeavor to plant a Sunday School wherever there is a population."[54] Highly concerned that no one miss an opportunity for biblical instruction, workers for the Union were encouraged to travel by foot. As a result of providing opportunity to study Scripture, the Union began publishing other works that would improve the life of its members. The society sold various books such as an alphabet primer, spelling books, and various volumes of Christian and cultural interest. The books sold by the Union became the growing nucleus of many libraries across the nation. In 1859, 60 percent of all American libraries were supplied by the Sunday School Union.[55]

The movement began to develop its own culture and influence. Tremendous loyalty developed toward the Sunday School with its key emphasis on lay leadership. Musically, it developed themes that reflect the times in which it flourished. For example, the famous song "Jesus Loves Me" appeared in a novel entitled *Say and Seal* published in 1860. The novel depicts the drama of a young Sunday School teacher and a dying Sunday School student. The teacher recites the comforting words of the hymn to the dying boy. Songs of the Sunday School often depicted such death motifs. This idea was in harmony with the high mortality rate among children, the view of the child as a small adult in need of conversion, and the frequent acquaintance with death in nineteenth-century society. Later with the American Civil War, Sunday School hymns reflected more military themes. For example, the hymn "Battle Hymn of the Republic" has a military motif. With new concern for the natural development of the child, songs were written describing the child's relationship to nature. For example, the "Sunbeam" songs are one example.[56] Sunday School became a highly identifiable cultural force in American life.

Organizational and educational change came into the Sunday School Movement following the American Civil War (1861-65). Because of the War, both the movement and denominations were split. Slowly, through the work of the Sunday School, unity across the nation in regard to the cause of Christ became more and more a reality. The Sunday School became a global work of evangelical Protestantism through the "Illinois Band" initially led by Dwight L. Moody, William Reynolds, Benjamin F. Jacobs, and John H. Vincent. Through brilliant organization, the International Sunday School Convention was formed in 1872. Jacobs developed a plan of dividing the various states and cities into districts for effective Sunday School work. These volunteer representatives met every three years for an international convention for promoting the work of the Sunday School.

In early Sunday School work, there was no uniformity in curriculum materials and the recruitment and training of teachers. Vincent began Sunday School teachers institutes as early as the 1860s. He proposed a uniform lesson plan to be used by all teachers in all evangelical

Protestant churches. At the 1872 convention, a committee was established to plan a uniform lesson scheme. Completed by 1876, the Uniform Lesson plans were established on a seven-year cycle. Each lesson would be studied by each person in Sunday School on a given Sunday. The Uniform Lessons provided a common language for evangelical Protestants.

These two ideas—the organization into districts and the use of uniform lessons—strengthened the Sunday School movement. The Sunday School in the late 1800s and early 1900s was a vital part of American life and ideal. The movement's popularity was felt in high levels of government. In 1910 President Taft hailed the Sunday School as necessary for the moral uplifting of the nation. Although it was raining, Congress was adjourned so its members could march in a parade celebrating the World's Sixth Sunday School Convention in 1910.[57]

The Sunday School Union and churches began to provide training opportunities for various ages. In 1874 at Lake Chautauqua, New York, a movement began that would have tremendous significance in the field of adult education, particularly for the education of Sunday School teachers. Vincent, first chairman of the International Sunday School Lesson committee, led in a brief summer course of two weeks for Sunday School workers. Over one thousand people attended this first Chautauqua meeting. The movement combined short study courses, popular lectures, recreation, and enthusiastic religious services. Later, in 1878, the movement became known as the Chautauqua Literary and Scientific Circle. This circle provided popular education through home reading in the sciences, literature, and other subjects.[58] With new interest in the developmental needs of adolescents, two new denominational groups were formed: the Methodist Epworth League and the Baptist Young People's Union.[59]

From 1916 to 1940, a decline occurred in the Sunday Schools, both in enrollment of pupils and the number of schools. Eavey offers various reasons for this decline. Theological liberalism weakened the belief in the need for salvation through Jesus Christ. The moral imperative and absolute were lost. Commitment was lost for the work of the

Sunday School. Church educators began to adopt the methods of the public schools which were based upon Greek ideals. However, such methods and inherent philosophy may not be congruent with Christian education. Church teachers hesitated to adopt new methods and materials. Older methods were retained, in spite of lack of interest and appeal. Church ecclesiastical structure limited the growth of Sunday School, seeking to preserve its own interests rather than granting the needed freedom in education. It became obvious that God's work with people may not always flourish within set denominational structures, practices, and restrictions.[60]

Robert Lynn and Elliott Wright argue that the Sunday School movement has been extremely successful because of high loyalty, ability to create its own liturgy, lay leadership, ownership, and involvement. These authors state:

> Succinctly put, the Sunday School is American Protestantism's training ground. Denominations have established hundreds of colleges and universities, but the Sunday School is the big school in matters religious for the Protestant people—originally and especially white people—though it has played a distinctive role in the religious experience and culture of black America. Compared to public education, Sunday School is marginal to American society, yet is an important little school in the rearing of the whole nation. The Sunday School is the big little school of the United States.[61]

Learning Activity 2.4

1. What is the significance of the Uniform Lessons for Protestants?
2. What is Chautauqua? What are some present-day expressions of the Chautauqua intent?
3. How are the Sunday School and the spirit of America related?

Common School Movement

Twentieth-century American education underwent significant changes brought about by the gradual transfer of denominational religious control to state and local government control, and the erosion of inherited social class distinctions brought about by the democratic process. The plea for a common universal education began to gain support in the United States because the concept of "common" involved shared ideas, experiences, goals, and beliefs of the community. Major educational leaders included Horace Mann, Henry Barnard, and James C. Carter.[62]

Horace Mann (1796-1859) persuaded reluctant Protestant clergy to support a common school that would nurture a common Christian morality: a nondenominational Protestantism. Mann regarded schools as agencies for nurturing socially moral citizens. Supported by the state and controlled by the public, schools should be accessible to all. Henry Barnard (1811-1900) believed that American education should strengthen economic individualism. Educated people would be more productive workers than ignorant people. A common element of Christianity would be passed on in the school system. State legislatures passed tax laws to support of public education. Later, public school education was extended to include secondary and higher education.[63]

Other Changing Expressions of Christian Education

After the American Civil War, a new secularization of education began. Institutional religion began to lose its leadership impetus in American education. Ministers became less numerous in the governing boards of universities and colleges and in positions of public education administration. Traditionally, college presidencies had been filled from those in Christian ministry. A layperson in the office of the president was a rarity before the beginning of the twentieth century. By 1898 Yale had its first lay president; in 1902 Princeton had its first lay president. By mid-twentieth century, the minister-president was the exception.

Religious controls over private education diminished and so did its influence in public education. In addition to an emphasis on Sunday School, other avenues of influence in public education were sought. Church weekday schools were established. Other groups conducted classes supplemental to the public schools, either in early morning, late afternoon, or during summer months. Some sought to divide a student's time between two schools or two teaching groups. Some groups sought to retain religion in public instruction while others focused attention on the church-related college.[64]

Various methods to provide religious instruction apart from the Sunday School developed. There was concern for the summer vacation time of students. In the early 1900s, the daily Vacation Bible School Movement began in New York City by an executive of the Baptist Mission Society. Soon other denominations showed an interest in special summer educational opportunities. In 1914 the Weekday Religious Education Movement began which involved release time, a designated time when students were released from regular academic studies to pursue religious instruction or activities. The practice of release time spread to various parts of the country. However, in 1948 the Supreme Court declared release time held in public schools unconstitutional. In 1952 release-time programs were declared legal if held away from school property and sponsored by and paid for by religious groups. Holding Sunday School on other days has only been marginally explored.[65]

Whereas the Catholic Church is more noted for establishing parochial schools, various non-Catholic groups such as Presbyterians and Lutherans have attempted to establish a system of schools under church control. The General Assembly of the Presbyterian Church in 1846 and 1847 approved a plan to establish a school in every congregation. While over 260 Presbyterian parochial schools were established, the system was abandoned in 1870. While not new, another focus of Christian education was supported by Horace Bushnell (1802-76). In 1861 Bushnell published *Christian Nurture*, which focused upon both evangelism and Christian education centering in the family. Although they showed interest, churches failed to adopt a family-centered type of Christian education. Churches were finding it hard to provide religious instruction in public schools, the family setting, and parochial schools; therefore, they turned their attention to the Sunday School.[66]

Professional educators entered the area of religious education with the goal of modernizing the Sunday School. In 1903 the Religious Education Association formed with the goal of transforming the Sunday School movement. In 1922 the International Council of Religious Education introduced the graded lessons that provided for lessons designed for each age level. In the 1930-40s these religious education professionals were attracted to liberal theology. The Religious Education movement failed to attract needed recruits and tended to alienate nonprofessional evangelicals.[67]

Baptists and Southern Baptists

Various denominations joined the Sunday School enterprise in an effort to adopt the Sunday School to their unique needs and beliefs. Two of the early denominations with this Sunday School interest were the Methodists and the Baptists. By 1826 churches showed initial interest in maintaining their own Sunday Schools in keeping with their doctrinal beliefs and practices, rather than taking a nonsectarian approach.[68] As early as 1844 the Baptist Conventions of Alabama, Georgia, Mississippi, Kentucky, and North Carolina began an organized effort of Sunday School promotion.[69]

The Southern Baptist Convention's first Sunday School Board was established in Greenville, South Carolina, in 1863. As part of its assignment, this group prepared lesson books, hymn books, question books, teachers' class books, and *The Sunday School Primer*. Because many children attending Sunday School could not read, *The Primer* contained simple reading exercises, spelling lessons, and Bible stories. Because of financial hardships, the board was dissolved in 1873. The Domestic (Home) Mission Board was given the responsibility of Sunday School promotion.[70]

Increasingly, Southern Baptists began to develop a comprehensive plan for designing literature, promoting the Sunday School organization, and equipping the local church ministries. In 1891 the Southern Baptist Convention voted to establish its present Sunday School

Board in Nashville, Tennessee, to publish and to promote the work of the Sunday School. In 1901 the Sunday School Board began hiring field workers to promote Sunday School work in various states. Its first field worker, Bernard W. Spilman, prepared books on the administration of the Sunday School. These books became the initial volumes in what would become the Church Study Course, a series of instructional materials designed to improve the leadership skills of church leaders in various ministry tasks.

One priority was to make the Sunday School "Baptist" in material and loyalty. Prior to this time, many Sunday Schools meeting in Southern Baptist churches were tied to non-Convention organizations. In 1905 the Board published *The Superintendent's Quarterly* that gave administrative suggestions and directions. This publication helped bring standardization of Sunday School activities in Southern Baptist churches. Increasingly concerned with training leadership, the Sunday School Board held its first major-city training session in Nashville in 1906. Subsequent city training schools developed into associational training schools. In 1908 Spilman helped secure a charter for Ridgecrest Baptist Assembly, a center for training workers. An additional training center developed at Glorieta, New Mexico.

In 1908 the Standard of Excellence was developed to guide Southern Baptist educational philosophy and organization. Requirements included church control of the Sunday School, use of the Bible as the text, and the use of Southern Baptist literature. Evangelism became a central part of the Southern Baptist Sunday School. Arthur Flake, a successful Sunday School worker, developed an early procedure for Sunday School growth. Known as Flake's formula, the five steps provided a model for organizing, training, and reaching individuals for Sunday School. Through a commitment to Sunday School and evangelism, Southern Baptists developed a highly sophisticated system of Sunday Schools with a large segment of its denomination involved in the support of Bible study and outreach.[71]

The Sunday School contributed significantly to the development of the largest Protestant denomination in the United States. William P.

Clemmons summarized the role of Sunday School to Southern Baptist churches:

> The Sunday School, therefore, among Southern Baptists is primarily a twentieth-century phenomenon, a relatively short period in which to evaluate its contributions. To churches, however, its contributions have been significant in the development of the largest Protestant denomination in the United States. The contribution can be noted especially in the areas of (1) growing an involved laity; (2) building a truly native Southern Baptist expression of church; (3) creating a means for rural Baptists in the South to make the transition to urban, affluent, educated and sophisticated mainline American Protestantism; (4) numerical and financial growth; and (5) redefining the work and role of professional clergy staffs in the churches.[72]

Learning Activity 2.5

1. What does common Christianity refer to in relation to the Common School Movement?
2. Describe various alternate approaches to Christian education, apart from Sunday School.
3. Examine your own Sunday School. What, if any, innovations might aid in achieving its objectives?
4. Brainstorm alternative practices or forms of Christian education.

The Church Today

The educational focus of the church in America today is diverse and widespread. Undergraduate degrees, as well as graduate degrees, train leaders in the field of Christian education. Various denominations support their own private schools from kindergarten through the graduate level. A high degree of professionalism has developed in the American setting of Christian education.

The nineteenth and twentieth centuries witnessed the rapid growth of private Christian schools. Various reasons may explain this growth. Faith in the public school system has been lost for some Protestant Evangelicals. While the American public school system was based upon common Christian values, the value system may not be operating effectively in today's public schools. Complaints range from mild displeasure to utter outrage. Complaints include immoral behavior, drug abuse, violence, low academics, lessened parental control of school, and heightened financial costs of public education. Protestant Evangelicals are concerned with the type of person the public school is producing.[73]

We live in a world of plurality and sophistication in respect to Christian education. Youth groups, parachurch groups, and private Bible study groups abound. Large numbers attend seminars and workshops as individuals seek to study the Word. Denominations publish vast amounts of literature for their constituencies. Christian education has become a vast enterprise.

Our world has changed through education and the media. First, the printing press allowed for the widespread availability of the Bible. This availability demanded reading. Beginning with the Reformation, education dramatically altered human development through the reading of the Word. Now television has revolutionized the world. Countless hours are spent before this "enlightening machine." Christian programming has become a widespread enterprise in addition to secular programming. Education and the media are powerful forces that influence personality and behavior.

What role should Christian education have today? Decisions must be made that will permit the creation of educational structures, either formal or informal, and allow for the realization of the Christian intent. What will that structure be?

Interestingly enough, readers of this book will determine what structures exist or do not exist in Christian education today. If ignored, deterioration may occur. If not addressed properly, structures not congruent with the Christian message may develop. If addressed properly, structures may foster the individual growth of the Christian and the corporate growth of the Christian church. Too often, means and ends are vague, and we go through various rituals without grasping the intent or the meaning.

While the reader may feel that an exhaustive journey has been made through thousands of years in the history of Christian education, only the tip of a great iceberg has been portrayed. Some of the highlights have been accented. Looking at the human struggle through history, the struggle may be summarized by the phrase "Quest for the Word." (See Figure 2.1)

In the beginning, human beings were created in the image of God and experienced perfect fellowship with God. Because of human disobedience, the human race was set out of that relationship. History records humanity's attempt to reestablish that void in life. God placed many indicators in the world to show humans of their need for Him. God sent His Son Jesus to reveal the Way. The Way was recorded in Holy Scriptures. The Scriptures pointed to human beings finding perfect fellowship with their Creator.

Once the Word was written, humanity had the all-sufficient guide for life. However, through ignorance and corruption, humankind lost the Word. Access to scripture became the privilege of only a few. One of the highlights of the Reformation was a renewed interest in the Bible and various efforts to translate the Bible into the vernacular languages. People needed instruction in how to read so that they could have the privilege of reading the Bible for themselves. Thus, the Word became the primary text for human beings in their search for a better life.

Today we live in a world in which we have access to the Word. We have school systems to teach us the reading skills necessary for reading the Word. We have well-developed churches that seek to instruct their members in the Word. Instruction in the Word has become a primary concern for the evangelical church today.

The study of history provides important lessons and insights for those concerned with the process of Christian education. Basic principles from history have been clearly illustrated. Such principles may form part of the needed biblical model for daily life and vision.

1. Biblical sources stress the importance of the family in the religious instruction of its members. While other organizations may pro-

MAN'S QUEST FOR THE WORD

**MAN
BEFORE THE FALL**

—perfect relationship
with the Word.
—Genesis 1:1

**MAN
AFTER THE FALL**

—broken relationship
with God and the Word

**MAN SEARCHES FOR
MEANING**

—searches in
the created order
for what he misses

MAN FINDS SIGNS

The Law
The Prophets
—gives evidence of the
Word

CHRIST

—the Word became
Flesh and dwelt
among us.
— John 1:14

EARLY CHURCH

—Scripture records
the Word
—open to all believers
through written and
spoken word

MIDDLE AGES

—Man loses the
Written Word
—masses of people
are uneducated
—Bible the property
of the educated clergy

**RENAISSANCE AND
REFORMATION**

—renewed interest in
learning
—Bible is placed in the
hands of the people

THE PRESENT

—the Word is available for all
—translations
—mass printings
—media

Figure 2.1

vide religious education, the family must not abandon its responsibility. Historically, the family has not taken its responsibility seriously.

2. Christian families have the responsibility for providing for religious training as well as skills and social training necessary for life. The Christian family's task is to nurture members in their relationship with God, the world, and others.

3. Christian education must center around Holy Scripture and its application to responsible daily living. The Word must become living Word in individual lives.

4. Christian education has the primary responsibility of nurturing disciples throughout the life span. The church must seek to equip all to be and make disciples.

5. Christian education is evangelistic in scope. To study and to evangelize are the fruits of the same plant.

6. All of life is the context for explaining the work of God. Christian education must seek to help the individual to explore the working of God in all arenas of life's concerns. God's work permeates all of the created order.

7. Christian educational institutions such as the church school, the private school, and the family must not forsake their theological and philosophical frameworks. To abandon our roots in the gospel is to be less than Christian in our educational endeavors.

8. The church must develop all avenues necessary to reach her people in the twentieth and twenty-first centuries. Traditions must be regarded as traditions. The responsibility for teaching the Bible must remain priority. Structure can be beneficial, but structure can be hindering to the task if it fails to carry out the biblical mandate.

9. All individuals, laity and professionals, must be involved in Christian education. The responsibility for teaching is not the exclusive domain of the professionally trained. One of the strengths of the Sunday School has been its lay leadership and sponsorship. One of the strengths and promises of Christian education occurs when the Bible is in the heart and hands of every individual. Scripture must remain the Book of the people in order that we may become people of the

Book.

10. Each generation of Christians must seek to preserve and to transmit Christian education. Failing to teach is failing to live responsibly. Careful analysis of what we teach, to whom we teach, and how we teach must occur continuously. Failure to teach is failure in discipleship.

Learning Activity 2.6

1. In your own words, summarize the history of Christian education. If you prefer, create a pictorial representation of the history of Christian education.
2. Describe what you imagine Christian education will be like in a hundred years.

Notes

1. Elmer Harrison Wilds and Kenneth V. Lottich, *The Foundations of Modern Education*, 4th ed. (New York: Holt, Rinehart and Winston, 1970), 212-13.
2. Thomas Hardy Leahey, *A History of Psychology: Main Currents in Psychological Thought*, 2d ed. (Englewood Cliffs, N.J.: Prentice-Hall, 1987), 79-80.
3. Wilds and Lottich, 211-13.
4. Gerald L. Gutek, *A History of the Western Educational Experience* (New York: Random House, 1972), 102-3.
5. Wilds and Lottich, 217-18.
6. Ibid., 218.
7. Gutek, 107-10.
8. Wilds and Lottich, 219.
9. Baker, *A Summary of Church History*, 198-99.
10. Kagan, Ozment, and Turner, 428.
11. Philip McNair, "Seeds of Renewal," *Eerdman's Handbook to the History of Christianity*, org. ed. Tim Dowley (Grand Rapids: Wm. B. Eerdmans Publishing Co., 1977), 352.
12. Kagan, Ozment, and Turner, 428.
13. Ibid., 428.
14. Good, 155-56.
15. Paul Monroe, *A Brief Course in the History of Education* (New York: MacMillan Co., 1907), 214.
16. Wilds and Lottich, 231-42.
17. G. R. Elton, *Reformation Europe: 1517-1559*, Fontana History of Europe, gen. ed. J. H. Plumb (Fontana, England: Collins, 1963), 290.
18. Eby, 71-79.

19. Lewis W. Spitz, *The Renaissance and Reformation Movements*, vol. 2, *The Reformation* (St. Louis: Concordia Publishing House, 1971), 347-48.
20. Gutek, 127.
21. Eby, 117.
22. Elton, 238.
23. Eavey, 163.
24. Gutek, 126.
25. Eavey, 151.
26. Eby, 120. William Stevenson, *The Story of the Reformation* (Richmond: John Knox Press, 1959), 170-71.
27. Gutek, 129-30.
28. Eavey, 152.
29. Elton, 205-6.
30. Eby, 109-14.
31. Elton, 205-6.
32. Eby, 114.
33. Elton, 205-6.
34. Spitz, 481.
35. Eby, 216-22.
36. Ibid., 223.
37. Ibid., 227.
38. Eavey, 190-93.
39. Raymond E. Callahan, *An Introduction to Education in American Society: A Text With Readings*, Foreword by George S. Counts (New York: Alfred A. Knopf, 1956), 116.
40. Eby, 239-43.
41. Ibid., 243.
42. Robert W. Lynn and Elliott Wright, *Big Little School: Two Hundred Years of Sunday School*, 2d ed. (Birmingham: Religious Education Press, 1980), 24-26.
43. Eby, 375-76.
44. Lynn and Wright, 36-37.
45. Eavey, 230.
46. Lynn and Wright, 63-64.
47. Eavey, 230.
48. Lynn E. May, Jr., "The Sunday School: A Two-Hundred-Year Heritage," *Baptist History and Heritage* 15 (October 1980): 3.
49. Eavey, 231-33.
50. Lynn and Wright, 40.
51. William W. Sweet, *The Story of Religion in America* (Grand Rapids: Baker Book House, 1950), 253.
52. Ibid., 254.
53. Eavey, 234.
54. Ibid., 234. Quotation from the Constitution of the American Sunday School Union.
55. Lynn and Wright, 52-57.

56. Ibid., 68-82.

57. Ibid., 94-115.

58. Eby, 595-96.

59. Lynn and Wright, 123.

60. Eavey, 266-69.

61. Lynn and Wright, 15-16.

62. Gutek, 359-60.

63. Ibid., 360-65.

64. Edwin Scott Gaustad, *A Religious History of America* (New York: Harper & Row, 1966), 372-73.

65. Lynn and Wright, 3-4.

66. Eavey, 251.

67. Lynn and Wright, 125-44.

68. Eavey, 251.

69. May, "The Sunday School: A Two-Hundred-Year Heritage," 4.

70. Lynn E. May, Jr., "The Emerging Role of Sunday Schools in Southern Baptist Life to 1900," *Baptist History and Heritage* 18 (January 1983): 6-15.

71. James E. Fitch, "Major Thrusts in Sunday School Development Since 1900," *Baptist History and Heritage* 18 (January 1983): 17-21.

72. William P. Clemmons, "The Contributions of the Sunday School to Southern Baptist Churches," *Baptist History and Heritage* 18 (January 1983): 31.

73. Paul Keinel, *The Christian School: Why It Is Right For Your Child* (Wheaton, Ill.: Victor Books, 1974), 27-32.

3
Theological and Philosophical Foundations for Christian Education

An Overview of the Relationship Theme

Christian education is integrally bound to its Christian theology and its philosophical concerns. To fail to acknowledge properly the educational, philosophical, and theological basis of Christian education is a grave disservice to Christian discipleship. Theological and philosophical issues must guide the formation of Christian education in its component areas of ontology, epistemology, axiology, learner, teacher, curriculum, methods, and outcome. Based upon these considerations, Christian education proceeds to reestablish human beings in their relationship to God, self, others, and the created order.

Theological Considerations

Which came first—the chicken or the egg? One confronts a similar question in attempting to deal with the historical, theological, and philosophical foundations of Christian education. The "ideal" would be to deal with all issues at once. Unfortunately, the reader, as well as the writer, would immediately experience sensory overload. Even following careful analysis, arbitrary or convenient plans are necessary. The initial chapters have covered the historical backgrounds; attention will now be given to the theological and philosophical foundations of Christian education. Discussion of specific philosophers is beyond the scope of this chapter. Selected discussions have been included in the chapter on historical foundations and will be included in the chapter on learning. While the treatment will be brief, theological and philosophical issues will be integrated and discussed throughout the remainder of the volume.

To survive, Christian education must establish its basis from its own theological antecedent. Too often, education that claims to be Christian has omitted important theological considerations; theological considerations form the basis of all Christian educational endeavors.

On occasion, some individuals have regarded Christian education as something devoid of theology or of a secondary importance in Christian ministry. Perhaps this accusation has been accurate in some practical expressions of Christian education. However, Christian education is integrally related to theology. Failing to acknowledge and express an understanding of Christian theology promotes an educational approach that is less than Christian. Christian education and Christian theology are partners in Christian discipleship. James S. Smart, in his classic work, *The Teaching Ministry of the Church*, states: "Educators must become theologians, for even the writer of the simplest Christian story for kindergarten children will go astray unless she understands the doctrine of the incarnation. And theologians must become educators."[1]

As a young undergraduate, this writer attended a local retreat where the leader spoke about a "new" aspect of theology. Until then, I thought theology consisted of a set of understandings or summary statements about the nature of God. To my rudimentary understanding of theology, the leader added the importance of "doing" theology. Clearly, the speaker gave to my "noun" approach to theology another dimension of a "verbal" (action) approach. Theology is both a summary statement of beliefs as well as a reflection of doing or life-style. The two are reflections or consequences of each other.

Interestingly, noted psychologist Alfred Adler spoke of a parallel situation in the dimension of belief and consequent attitude. According to Adler, each individual is born with a feeling of inferiority. As a result the individual begins to develop a life-style that seeks to overcome this feeling of inferiority or that is a quest for superiority. What we believe is reflected in our behavioral patterns. In comparison, what is believed theologically reveals itself in both attitude toward the world and action in the world.

To understand the critical relationship between theology and Christian education, it is necessary to explore the term *theology*. Theology is similar in concept to the idea of medicine. Just as medicine is a broad discipline with many different types of medicine involved, theology is a broad discipline with many types of theology. In carrying the analogy between medicine and theology one step further, we practice theology, just as we practice medicine. Theology may refer to various aspects including doctrinal teaching, the discipline of theology, and the various schools of theologies. In light of doctrine, theology includes Christology (Christ), anthropology (man), soteriology (salvation), ecclesiology (church), eschatology (last times), and Pneumatology (Holy Spirit).

Theology exists because God revealed Himself to humanity. Three primary sources of theology are the Old Testament, the New Testament, and church history. One basic function of theology is to serve as a guide for what we do educationally. Theology expresses what we believe based upon God's revelation. Theology ultimately demonstrates how to live in relationship to God, to our neighbor, to our world, and to ourselves. In order to determine one's theology, careful study of Scripture must take priority. Discovering what one believes about Scripture and the areas it addresses is not an easy task. Often, individual interpretations—the product of culture, history, and personal predispositions—become so intertwined with our view of the biblical revelation that it is difficult to separate the two.

One must develop tools for discovering what the biblical revelation involves. These tools are principles called hermeneutics—the process by which we interpret the Bible. Another ingredient is the consistency with which we apply those hermeneutical tools. Ultimately, because the Bible is divinely inspired, the Bible must be divinely interpreted. The Holy Spirit must guide in revealing Scripture.

Often we see examples of this guidance in daily Bible readings. Individuals may read a passage any number of times without any new or exciting relevancy. However, at times one reads the same familiar passage and receives a new, dynamic message. In effect, the passage may "speak" in a novel and powerful way. What brings about this sudden and new revelation? Various factors lead to this experience, including the particulars of a given situation, the needs of the individual at this particular time, or the work of the Holy Spirit. It may involve all three. Again the Holy Spirit is actively at work in the world providing comfort, guidance, and provision for the work of the church. Only through the Holy Spirit's direction can the message be understood and acted upon.

Hermeneutical tools include asking the basic questions of what the passage meant to its original audience and what it means to today's audience. There is a real sense in which theology must be reinterpreted to each new generation. Faith itself must be reinterpreted with each new generation. If not, faith lacks vibrancy, relevancy, and genuine meaning. If faith is not transmitted from one generation to the next, faith will die with the previous generation. Unless each generation discovers its meaning, the faith will be lost.

Learning Activity 3.1

1. Write in your own words what "theology" means.
2. List any "theologies" that you might know. What are the implications, if any, of these theologies for daily life?
3. Imagine that you have been asked to speak to a class of young Christians about "How to study the Bible." What tools or hermeneutical principles would you share with them? For example, how should they go about interpreting a passage of Scripture?
4. Theological Analysis. On a sheet of paper, list as many ideas as you can regarding practices or beliefs that you have about the Christian life. On the other half of the paper, list the source of each idea. For example, did you learn this idea from your church, from Bible study, or from your family background? Use this exercise to begin to determine the source of your beliefs. Are your beliefs totally

based upon the Bible? Are any beliefs based upon culture, family, or tradition?

In missiology, or the study of missions, the principle of trying to separate "essential" or "biblical" Christianity from cultural adornments becomes easily apparent. One vivid illustration compares carrying the gospel (the plant) in a container (representing the cultural-bound attributes of the planter) to the native soil of a foreign land (the recipient of the gospel). The planter or missionary must break the container (thereby seeking to rid the gospel of cultural bias) and plant the gospel in the native soil. In the process, the gospel will develop in the life-style of the new believer. Behavior changes and practices that occur will do so in light of the Holy Spirit's work in the lives of the believers. The message of redemption is transmitted without any cultural biases, restrictions, or prejudices.

2 Timothy 3:16-17 expresses the authority of Scripture. The passage states, "All Scripture is inspired by God and profitable for teaching, for reproof, for correction, and for training in righteousness, that the man of God may be complete, equipped for every good work." Scripture is the only record that we possess that will equip us for finding our life's potential as a servant of God. Regardless of our technological skills, unless we have training in righteousness, our work is incomplete or in vain. The purpose of the written revelation is to provide instruction for human beings in terms of salvation. Salvation involves our relationship with God. Consequently, other relationships with self, others, and the world change because of this new relationship with God. Scripture teaches how to live in accordance with God's will in all of life's dimensions.

Each individual involved in Christian education must be trained and involved in the study of God's Word. The assumptions and the conclusions drawn from such study shape the direction of life and practice of Christian education. Too often, models or world views different from a biblical model have been used by Christian educators. Consequently, these practitioners may have pursued goals or directed activities in ways contrary to the interest of the gospel and people.

Theology involves both an understanding of God's work and a response to that understanding. While there are various branches of theology, each branch seeks to provide descriptive statements and consequent implications for life. Christology involves the study of the nature and work of Christ. Anthropology involves the study of humankind as revealed in Scripture. Soteriology involves the study of the process of salvation, including conviction, justification, sanctification, and glorification. Ecclesiology involves the study of the structure and relationships found within the church. Eschatology involves the study of the last times. Pneumatology involves the study of the nature and work of the Holy Spirit. (See Figure 3.1).

Each of these areas has impact upon the practice of Christian education. To understand the significance of this information, one must remember that each study provides information regarding various facets of our life. As will be discussed in later chapters, human beings have four directions of relationships in which they are involved. These four include relationship toward God, toward others, toward self, and toward the world. Each area of theology provides insight into these relationship directions.

Theology and Christian education cannot be divorced. To do so is to make Christian education less than Christian and to make theology less than its intent. Christian education involves nurture or instruction in each area of theology. Christian education seeks to keep theology alive and transmitted from one generation to the next. Theology seeks to keep Christian education in line with biblical roots and practices. By necessity, each theologian is a Christian educator; each Christian educator is a theologian. (See Figure 3.2).

We cannot help but to convey theology. Every Christian is a theologian. Every Christian is a teacher. The questions remain: what type of theologians, and what type of Christian educators are we?

THEOLOGICAL BRANCHES AND THEIR RELATIONAL CONCERNS

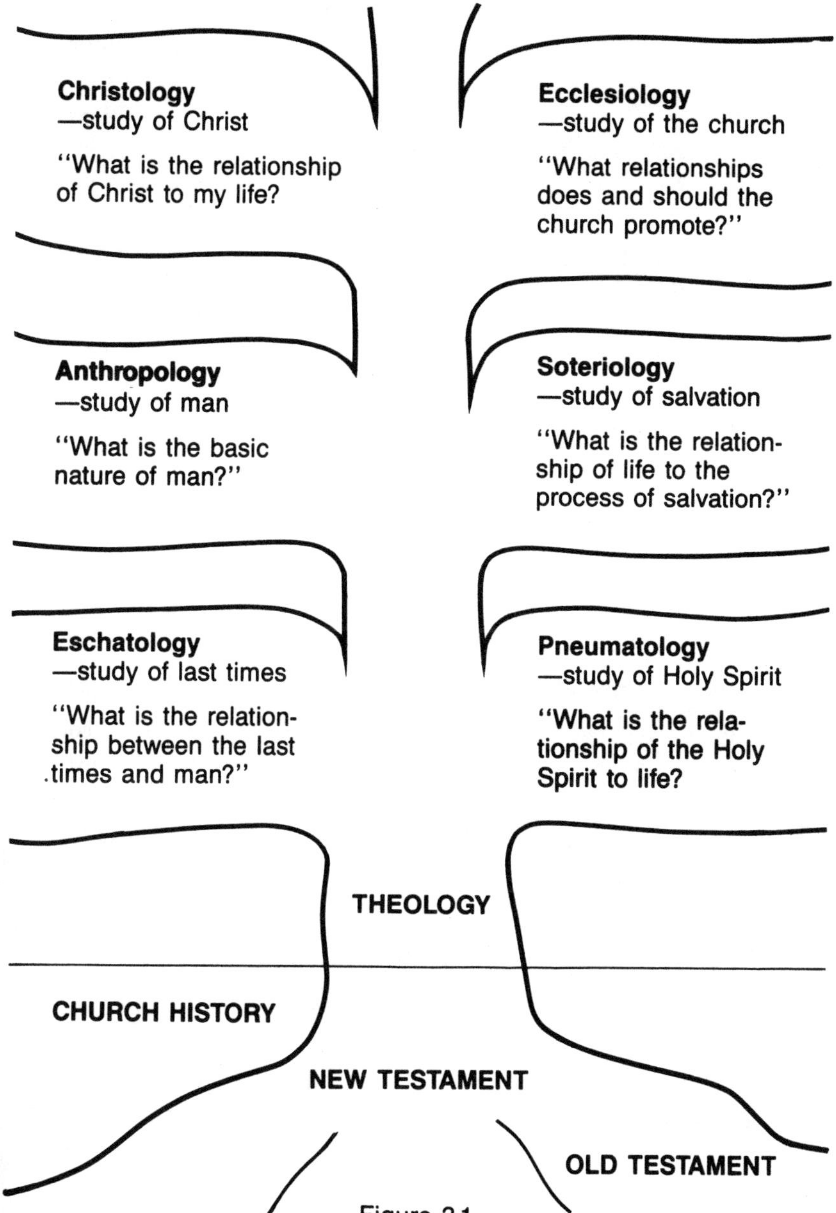

Christology
—study of Christ

"What is the relationship of Christ to my life?

Ecclesiology
—study of the church

"What relationships does and should the church promote?"

Anthropology
—study of man

"What is the basic nature of man?"

Soteriology
—study of salvation

"What is the relationship of life to the process of salvation?"

Eschatology
—study of last times

"What is the relationship between the last .times and man?"

Pneumatology
—study of Holy Spirit

"What is the relationship of the Holy Spirit to life?

THEOLOGY

CHURCH HISTORY

NEW TESTAMENT

OLD TESTAMENT

Figure 3.1

CHRISTIAN EDUCATION AND CHRISTIAN THEOLOGY: REFLECTIONS OF EACH OTHER

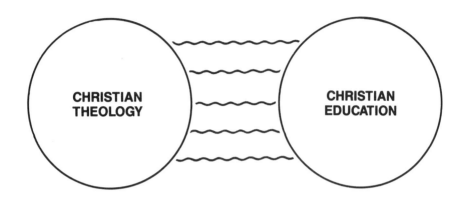

Figure 3.2

Learning Activity 3.2

1. Match the following branches of theology with their "best" corresponding definition.

   _____ 1. Christology   a. study of humankind
   _____ 2. Eschatology   b. study of salvation
   _____ 3. Ecclesiology   c. study of the last
                                          times
   _____ 4. Soteriology   d. study of Christ
   _____ 5. Anthropology   e. study of the church

2. Using the five branches of theology listed above, engage in more in-depth Bible study. Using each of these topics and a concordance, look up Scripture references and teachings for as many as you can find. For example, under ecclesiology, look up the word *church* in your concordance. Summarize your findings.

EDUCATIONAL PHILOSOPHICAL CONCERNS

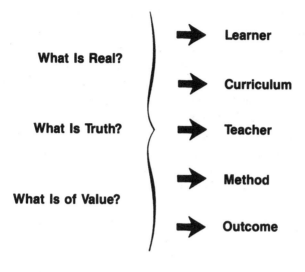

Figure 3.3

Philospohical Foundations

The word *philosophy,* or the love of wisdom, elicits many different meanings for individuals. Some of us love the discussion involved with philosophical issues; others are completely indifferent, or seemingly so, to the issues of philosophy. Regardless of our preference, philosophy is an area in which all are compelled to be involved to a degree. Whether we acknowledge it or not, all of us are influenced by philosophy. We are all practicing philosophers.

Philosophy involves the study of questions. What we do and what we feel are often a result of the answers given to various philosophical questions. At times, our philosophies are clearly explicit; at other times they are vaguely implicit. Whether we like it or not, philosophy is with us. Understanding our own philosophy is important because all of our actions reflect some philosophical position. How do our educational/theological actions relate to our basic philosophical positions? Philosophical questions typically raised in education center around the themes or topics of ontology, epistemology, axiology, the learner, curriculum, methods, the teacher, and social policy.[2]

As we begin to explore these topics, it is important to reexamine what we mean by the term *education*. Two possible Latin roots exist. "Educere" means to lead from, to draw out of. "Educare" means to mature, to rear, to raise. One's definition may depend upon whether one views the act as bringing out of the individual what nature cannot accomplish, or if one views the act as merely cooperating with nature's unfolding. One's definition (understanding) of education influences one's practice.

Christian education is not simply an isolated set of procedures or instructional methods. While procedures and methods must exist, these must be congruent with the theological or philosophical questions behind the actions. Those engaged in Christian education are not mere technicians. Indeed, they are theologians and practical appliers of the Word. In the fullest sense, theology reflects knowledge, understanding, life-style change, and an imperative to share the "good news." Anything less reflects a poor or immaturely developed theology.

The Issues

Philosophically, several issues or questions must be answered with regard to the practice of Christian education. Each of these eight areas involves countless questions. Each question leads to other questions and applications. The following discussions contain suggested questions to aid the reader in understanding the various problems to be addressed in Christian education.

Ontology concerns itself with what is real. Is life in the present the only entity that is real? If so, then what is the focus of education? If there is life beyond this moment, then what would the focus of education be? If both possibilities are real, then what should the focus of education be? Does reality change? If so, what impact does this have upon theology and, subsequently, on Christian education? Before one begins any educational quest, one must first decide what is real. Conceptions of reality guide subsequent behavioral pursuits.

Epistemology concerns itself with what is truth or what is knowledge. Is truth or knowledge complete or incomplete? What are the sources of truth or knowledge? What are the authorities of knowledge or truth? What elements of truth, if any, does science contain? Is knowledge or truth only to be found in God? How one regards truth or knowledge will impact the seeking of truth and the imparting of knowledge.

Axiology concerns itself with what is of value. What criteria is used to assess value? What is the value of the past, the present and the future? What value does Christian education have? Is it worthwhile for all age groups to receive instruction? Does our verbally expressed value to Christian education reflect the actual time, money, and talent devoted to its practice? What is important in a plan of church education? What is of importance in a plan of individual Christian education? How does one prioritize what needs to be taught? Such suggested questions demand answers. Values impact our ideas as well as our practice of Christian education.

Learning Activity 3.3

1. Write a brief definition for the following three terms:
a. epistemology: _____
b. axiology: _____
c. ontology: _____
2. Summarize briefly what you believe about each of the following.
a. epistemology: _____
b. axiology: _____
c. ontology: _____

Learner.—Do we possess a dynamic or a passive view of the learner? Our answers reflect how and what we teach. Does the learner actively get involved in the learning? Are the experiences of the learner important? What are the needs of the learner? If learners have special needs, does this require a different focus or adaptation of the Christian curriculum?

At what age does learning begin? What age marks the end of learning? How does intelligence or the ability to learn change over the life span? If change in learning ability occurs, how can Christian education adapt to meet the new needs and abilities? What is the impact of heredity and environment upon the learner? Will the learner develop into the fullest potential without outside intervention? Is humanity basically good, evil, or both? Our basic assumptions of human beings will influence our practice of their Christian education.

Teacher.—What is the role of the teacher in the educative process? Is the teacher an authority figure? Is the teacher a co-leader? Are there special innate qualities the teacher must possess? Is there a particular set of acquired information that the teacher must possess before beginning to teach? Are different types of teachers needed for different age groups? If so, what are those qualities?

What type of training is needed for the teacher? What type of relationship should the teacher have with those whom he or she teaches? Various philosophies propose differing viewpoints of the teacher. What is your philosophy regarding the teacher? Are all Christians teachers?

Curriculum.—What is the role of the Bible in the curriculum? Are there additional significant documents in Christian education? Where does Christian education occur? What is the significance of life experiences and curriculum? Should the curriculum reflect only library study? Should the curriculum be experienced in the outside world beyond the church building? As one is involved in Christian curriculum development, these types of educational questions must be analyzed.

Methods.—What methods are appropriate to Christian education? Are methods related to age group? Do methods contribute to the message they seek to illustrate? Can the method chosen actually repudiate the message being taught? Are certain methods inappropriate for practice of Christian education? Are principles of behavior modification appropriate in the field of Christian education? What about library research? How much time is actually being devoted to Bible teaching in the typical Sunday School "hour?" Methodological practices emerge as an outgrowth of philosophical assumptions.

Outcome.—What is the outcome or the goal of the Christian educative process? Does Christian education seek to train individuals who repeat previously acquired dogma? Does Christian education seek to develop learners who apply Christian truth in daily life? Is our goal conversion? How does Christian education influence individuals in their relationships with others? Is there any type of missionary imperative within Christian education? Beginning with philosophical questions and assumptions, the process culminates in the product of Christian education—the Christian individual.

Those who pursue leadership in Christian education must consciously struggle with the answers to these and other questions. Once answers have been achieved, Christian education may be guided in a coherent fashion, not in a hit-or-miss enterprise. The reader must decide these issues, and they should not be dismissed without careful analysis.

Learning Activity 3.4

1. A. Think about two of the most influential or significant teachers that you have had. Choose one from a school context and the other from a church context. Describe each one. What are the similarities? What are the differences? What made each one significant or influential to you.

OR

1. B. Using the following outline, analyze those two teachers in light of their beliefs and actions about:
   1. Learner (pupil):
   2. Teacher:
   3. Curriculum:
   4. Methods:
   5. Outcome:

2. If you are a teacher, list what you believe to be summary statements about the following. Describe how you "practice" your belief.

Belief: *Practice:*

1. Learner:

2. Teacher:

3. Curriculum:

4. Method:

5. Outcome:

3. Imagine that you are one of your own learners or students. How would your students fill out the chart based upon what you say and what you do?

Belief: *Practice:*

1. Learner:

2. Teacher:

3. Curriculum:

4. Method:

5. Outcome:

A Theological/Philosophical Model

This chapter has focused on the integral nature of theology, philosophy, and Christian education. Developing a view of education that incorporates a biblical position is essential. Various questions have been posed for the readers, and the readers must formulate their own ideas regarding the nature of theology and philosophy to the practice of Christian education. This formulation will involve continued reappraisal and reevaluation. The views we form will become the basis of what we teach, how we teach, whom we teach and for what intent we teach.

The following model depicts a relationship view of Christian education. It will be discussed throughout the remainder of the work where appropriate.

Ontology (Reality):

1. The world is created and sustained by God.
2. The world is subject to natural laws established by God.
3. As a creation of God, the world is still subject to supernatural intervention by God.
4. The world attests, through various natural observations, a created order and Creator.
5. Reality is held together by Jesus Christ, the Son of God. Christ was crucified and resurrected on our behalf. To those who believe on Him, eternal life is promised.
6. Reality exists on a present level and a future level.
7. Life lived is done so in relationship to the demands of reality.

Epistemology (Truth or Knowledge):

1. God reveals Himself through both natural and special revelation.
2. Knowledge may thus be gained through both natural and special revelation.
3. Special revelation includes the Bible, prayer, and the work of the Holy Spirit.
4. All knowledge or truth belongs to God. True knowledge from one arena will not contradict another arena.
5. The Bible explans to human beings their relationship with God, themselves, and others.
6. The curriculum or knowledge to be studied should include the world because the world is a part of God's creation.
7. Methods or means used to obtain knowledge must be appropriate

to the area under investigation. Different disciplines will require different methodologies.

Axiology (Value):

1. All of life is to be valued.
2. Each individual has inherent worth because of being created in the image of God. Individual differences are to be appreciated and developed.
3. Community and relationships are to be valued.
4. Values emerge in light of ontological and epistemological questions and answers.

Learner:

1. Human beings are created in the "image of God" and from the "dust of the ground." Humans are like the other creatures in their kinship and yet different because they are created in the image of God.
2. Because of sin, the human race and the world have fallen from God's original purpose. Therefore, each human being is in need of personal redemption.
3. Human beings have individual differences. While all are created in the image of God, each individual, because of basic temperament, sin, or societal influences, may lead a life near or far from God's plan.
4. God in the person of Jesus Christ has redeemed those who confess their faith in Him.
5. Human beings who have accepted Christ as Lord and Savior enter a process of growth and maturation toward finding their redeemed and recreated selves. Because each person is an individual, each pilgrimage will be somewhat different.
6. While people are responsible for their acceptance of Christ, each person is also responsible for his or her commitment to growth and maturity.

Teacher:

1. Being a Christian involves being a sharer of the faith (a teacher) with those both in and out of the faith.
2. All Christians are teachers in either a formal or an informal sense.
3. By living example, the teacher should demonstrate the qualities sought in Christian example.

Curriculum:

1. The curriculum consists of the Holy Scriptures and the life concerns of the individual.
2. The world itself is the classroom in which scriptural truth may be experienced.
3. The curriculum addresses the four basic relationships of the human race: God, self, others, and the created order.
4. The curriculum seeks to develop the giftedness of each individual.

Method:

1. Any method may be chosen that is consistent with Scripture, the needs and interests of the learner, and the basic nature of the material's content.
2. Methodology is the means to aid in the end process of Christian discipleship.

Outcome:

1. The goal is to produce stewards who acknowledge their giftedness in service to God.
2. Stewardship will reveal itself in four basic life-style relationships: God, self, others, and the created world.

Learning Activity 3.5

1. Draw a diagram to illustrate the relationship between theology and Christian education.
2. Examine the current Christian educational system of which you are a part. (This may be a college, seminary, or your own local

church.) What ideas does this system promote by its actions with regard to philosophical and theological issues? Is this system consistent with your own beliefs and theological convictions? Explain.

Notes

1. James S. Smart, *The Teaching Ministry of the Church: An Examination of the Basic Principles of Christian Education* (Philadelphia: The Westminster Press, 1964), 66.

2. For an in-depth consideration of philosophical issues, see J. Donald Butler, *Four Philosophies and Their Practice in Education and Religion*, 3d ed. (New York: Harper & Row Publishers, 1968).

Part II:

Toward a Practice of Christian Education

4

A View of Christian Learning

An Overview of the Relationship Theme

Questions concerning human nature and how human beings learn may be traced back to the ancient Greeks. Initially, questions about learning were explored from a philosophical position. The issues of nature and nurture have formed an ever-enduring debate since the early Greeks. Modern psychology and modern learning theory were born with the wedding of the questions of philosophy and the discoveries of physiology. Issues of learning could be explored scientifically. Various modern theories emerged that labeled a person as an organism composed of stimulus-response bonds; other theories explained a human being as a thinking organism. Each learning theory has its own philosophical presuppositions from which it operates. What we think about mankind determines how we view and guide learning. What we think about the human race determines how we will relate to human beings.

Relationship learning involves guiding human beings in their relationship to God, self, others, and the created order. Based upon biblical foundations, this theory seeks to aid humanity in finding proper stewardship relationships in these areas. Christian learning involves four domains: knowledge, understanding, attitude, and performance. While we teach in any one area, we influence all other areas.

Christian learning should begin with a therapeutic core comprised of empathy, congruence, unconditional positive regard, and the Holy Spirit. The Holy Spirit allows for this bridge of relationships to be established. Christian learning involves: (1) a mature confrontation that stimulates and guides growth; (2) a shared recognition of individual giftedness; (3) an intergenerational relationship that guides continuous sharing of the faith; (4) the use of symbols which accurately express our relationships; (5) the context and method which includes human beings, their world, and the truth of Scripture; and (6) the continuous integration of the faith into all areas of life. The end result of learning should be a faithful steward of all God's blessings.

One of the most explored areas in the field of psychology is learning theory. While modern psychology is a recent phenomenon, questions of psychology, especially about learning, have been explored for thousands of years. These questions were analyzed chiefly through philosophical speculations, and more questions have been raised about learning than have definitely been answered. Learning theory continues to be an important discipline of study and exploration.

Described in its global context, learning is the process by which individuals acquire a repertoire of skills, information, competencies, and attitudes. One characteristic that distinguishes humans from the animals is their vast capacity for learning. Learning has several distinctive values for humanity. Benefiting both the individual and society, learning allows for the transmission of knowledge from one generation to the next. Additionally, learning theory assists in understanding the motivation behind behaviors. The study of learning aids in understanding the process that produces both adaptive as well as maladaptive behavior.

Learning theory has definite application in almost every aspect of life. Knowing what contributes to adaptive and maladaptive behavior can have impact upon specific practices of psychotherapy. Practices of childrearing are influenced by findings in learning theory. Lastly, a close relationship exists between principles of learning and educational practices.

Learning theory has consequences for the specific practices of Christian education. As in philosophy, we operate under a given set of learning principles. These principles may be precisely articulated or vaguely felt. Regardless, the learning principles reveal themselves in specific actions. As illustrated in educational history and philosophy, practices of Christian education have often emerged from the social context. This chapter explores precursors of modern learning theories, summarizes major modern learning theories, and presents a theory of Christian learning based upon an understanding of the basic process.

Precursors to Modern Learning Theory

Early Greeks

While modern learning theory is relatively young in comparison to other disciplines, the concerns of learning theory can be traced back to early recorded history. In Western civilization, we often trace our philosophical questions to the early Greeks. Such is the case with learning theory. Various philosophical questions asked include: How do we know? How do we know that we know? How can we account for individual differences? What is the role of nature in learning? What is the role of environment in learning? One early Greek philosopher who explored learning theory was Empedocles of Acragas (450 B.C.), a physician-philosopher regarded as the founder of empiricism. According to Empedocles, objects emit "effluences" which are characteristics of the objects themselves. After the individual has experienced through his senses these objects, these effluences enter the bloodstream where they mix in the heart. Thinking is the vibration of the effluences in the beating of the heart. Thus, we know reality by observing it and then by internalizing copies of the object.[1]

One of the most familiar Greek philosophers, Plato (428-348 B.C.), dealt with the same issue of how ideas enter the mind. His work illustrates the enduring controversy regarding the battle between nature and nurture, or heredity and environment. Plato advocated that humans at birth possess vague and indistinct replicas of perfect laws. In the transition between the other world and the current world, these laws were dimmed in terms of their perfection. Human growth and development consists of the gradual unfolding of latent capacities within the individual. The environment provides sensations which arouse the corresponding ideas within the individual. These aroused ideas result in new knowledge or learning.

Plato's basic position was that of heredity; learning is inborn, waiting to be realized. Plato and his teacher Socrates spoke about memories as experiences recorded like wax impressions. The durability of the impression depends upon the frequency of the experience and the quality of the wax.

Plato's student, Aristotle (384-322 B.C.), believed that individual reality exists in the physical world. Learning comes about through contact with the physical. Gaining knowledge is a psychological process that begins with the perception of particulars and ends with the general knowledge of universals. The body has special senses that passively receive the sensations emitted by external objects. Each special sense corresponds only with certain qualities that it can perceive. For example, only vision can perceive color; only taste can perceive sweetness. Another element called "common sense" unifies data from the special sense into a coherent, conscious experience. Aristotle gave the term *mind* to the rational part of human souls. Unique to human beings, the mind allows for the acquiring knowledge of abstract principles or generalities.

As we experience different impressions of the same natural type, we note similarities and form an impression of the universal. For example, after experiencing a multitude of cats, one begins to form an idea of what a cat is. The mind is composed of two parts: the passive and the active. Knowledge of the universal occurs in the passive mind that is acted upon by the active mind. This active mind is pure thought. According to Aristotle, the active mind is unchangeable and immortal.

Memory is a library consisting of a set of images that represent past experiences. Because memory is organized, recollection or retrieval is possible. The organization is based upon the association of ideas or images. Four kinds of connections exist between ideas: contiguity of one idea with another idea, series of ideas, similarity of ideas, and contrast of ideas. Varied sense experiences allow for the creation of memory and its retrieval.

Aristotle's ideas were taught and believed until the Middle Ages. The stage was set for debate between the question of nature versus nurture and heredity verses environment. While both theorists acknowledged the importance of the mind, Plato's emphasis was heredity with knowledge as innate, and Aristotle's emphasis was environment with knowledge gained through environmental or sensory contact.[2]

Another significant individual in light of learning theory is Saint Augustine (A.D. 354-430). The early Christians believed that knowledge begins first with faith, which then leads to a transcendental awareness of God. For the Platonists, reason is the light of learning; for the Christian, faith is the light of learning.[3]

Augustine is credited with being the last classic philosopher and the first Christian one. Augustine synthesized faith and philosophy into a Christian world view that would dominate European thought until the thirteenth century. Under Augustine's influence, philosophical speculation was centered in the context of the Christian faith. Rather than focusing upon observing the external world, Augustine's followers focused upon introspecting the world beyond. All of life must be approached through the eyes of faith.[4]

Scholasticism

Medieval scholasticism sought a synthesis of all knowledge. Because all knowledge was of God, it was believed that knowledge, tradition, and faith could be synthesized into a single, grand, authoritative picture of the universe. Saint Thomas Aquinas's (1225-74) *Summa Theologia* represents such an attempt. Aquinas advocated the reconciliation of the teachings of the church and the findings of naturalism and believed there were limits to an individual's knowledge of the world. Aquinas endeavored to harmonize Aristotle's empiricism and the Christian faith. According to Aquinas, faith and reason are compatible.

Scholastics explored the issue of realism versus nominalism. Realists like Aquinas believed that universal ideas exist independently and prior to individual objects. If carried to an extreme, realism would require the rejection of the material world. Nominalism insists that universals are created by reason. Led by William of Ockham (1300-49), nominalism taught that mental realities are universals only in so far as they stand for the many. According to Ockham, all knowledge is possible through the intellect.[5]

Scholastic psychology contributed to learning theory by its explorations of the biological functions of learning, memory, and language. A difference exists between factual knowledge gained through the senses and the knowledge of principles known only by reason. While animals survive only by instinctual patterns, humans possess the ability to comprehend universals. Humans have an agent-intellect that abstracts the form of a thing from its appearance. While the senses can only deal with the characteristics, the intellect can abstract the form. Human knowledge is imperfect because human reason alone cannot comprehend the divine essence. Because there are differences in learning capacity among individuals, Scholastics acknowledged that some individuals are more prepared to lead and others more prepared to follow. One of the guiding maxims through the thirteenth and fourteenth century was the belief that nothing was in the intellect that was not first in the senses.[6] The work of the Scholastics laid the foundations for the birth of modern science.

The spirit of seventeenth-century Europe paved the way for the birth of modern psychology in the nineteenth century. The world, as well as the human race, was viewed as a great working machine. One of the primary leaders during this period was Rene Descartes (1596-1650). With his famous statement, "Cogito ergo sum" ("I think, therefore I am"), Descartes gave high emphasis to the importance of the rational aspects of human beings. Descartes began to explore the issues of philosophy through psychological introspection. Rather than pouring over ancient texts, philosophy was now to concern itself with an analysis of mind or experience. In addition, Descartes emphasized a mechanical concept of the world. God created a perfect machine and set it in motion. Human ability to reason allows one to understand these natural laws. Descartes proposed the dualism of mind and body. These two entities interact.[7]

The importance of the senses and the environment was carried on in the work of John Locke (1632-1704). Locke believed that experience and sensation were extremely important in the development of the individual. In fact, the individual is born with a blank slate or "tabula rasa." The mind is composed of connections or association of ideas. Continuing this idea, David Hume (1711-76) believed that ideas were sensations. He believed that one set of sensations became associated with another set; the first set possessed the power to call into memory the second set.

Other philosophers and researchers would continue this thread of the association or connection between ideas. David Hartley (1705-57) reduced ideas to sensations and sensations to nerve vibrations. James Mill (1773-1836) stressed that association of ideas was the mental corresponding or the simple addition of elements.[8] Johann Herbart (1776-1841) dealt with learning the new in terms of the old *apperception*. Once ideas and sensations enter the mind, they remain there to influence future learning. John Stuart Mill (1806-73) developed the laws of association of ideas—similarity, contiguity, frequency, and inseparability. These theorists have each contributed to the development of modern learning theory.

A German experimentalist, Hermann Ebbinghaus (1850-1909), made the first systematic laboratory study of learning. He conducted the first thoroughly scientific study of learning by association. From Empedocles to Ebbinghaus, the theory of learning had progressed from early philosophical speculations to the modern age of psychological research. The early Greeks focused upon the association of ideas. Modern psychology focused instead on the association or connection between various physiological or nervous system imprints.[9]

Various advances in experimental physiology contributed to the development of modern learning theory. Johannes Muller (1801-58) began the scientific study of sensory nerves, studying the specific energies of nerves. Marshall Hall (1790-1857), studying reflex behavior, concluded that various parts of the brain and the nervous system are responsible for various behaviors. Pierre Flourens (1794-1867) studied various functions of the brain and spinal column. These individuals are representative of those that contributed to the scientific study of psychology.[10]

Learning Activity 4.1

(Fill-in-the-Blanks)

1. Our ideas about modern learning theory are often traced to the Greeks. Early Greek philosophy was often divided in its viewpoints on the role of heredity and environment in learning. Whereas Socrates emphasized _____ as the more important element in learning, Plato emphasized _____ as the more important element in learning.
2. Augustine held that all of life must be examined through introspection or through the eyes of _____.
3. The thirteenth and fourteenth centuries held the belief that nothing existed in the _____ that was not first in the _____.

Modern Learning Theories

Structuralism.—The parents of modern psychology are said to be philosophy and physiology. Philosophers asked many questions about how humans acquired knowledge and the content of that knowledge; advances in physiology allowed for the exploration of bodily processes in a scientific sense. Modern psychology arose as a result of these philosophical questions and advances in experimental physiology.

Modern psychology began with Wilhelm Wundt (1832-1920) in 1879 in Leipzig, Germany. In this setting, Wundt established the first psychological laboratory. Seeking to gain credibility for psychology as a science, Wundt believed that psychology should focus exclusively on conscious experience, rather than unconscious experience. Conscious experiences could be measured; consequently, this approach would achieve more scientific credibility. Having come into the scientific arena late, psychology must devote itself to the predominant method used in the other sciences. Wundt's type of study became known as Structuralism, in which the investigator sought to identify the basic structure of the mind or experience. The goal was to create a periodic chart of the mind similar to the one that chemistry was producing of the elements.

Wundt's chief method of acquiring information was called introspection, which involved observing and reporting of conscious experience. This observation and reporting was done within the strictest scientific conditions. The vocabulary used to describe the experience must be sensate in content. For example, if shown a blue notebook, the experimenter would not report seeing a blue notebook. Instead, the experimenter would report on the blue sensations.

The work of Wundt attracted worldwide attention. Students came from various parts of Europe and North America to study with him. One of his British students, Edward Bradford Titchener (1867-1927), came to America and perpetuated the American version of structuralism. Teaching at Cornell University, Titchener emphasized the mechanistic spirit of structuralism. His subjects became merely recording agents of their own experiences. In addition, Titchener objected to any practical application of his investigation. Knowledge for the sake of knowledge was his exclusive concern.

Functionalism.—From the beginning, various leaders in psychology acted and reacted to the accomplishments and directions of Wundt and Titchener. In keeping with the American spirit of usefulness or practicality, one American reaction was led by William James (1842-1910). The question was no longer: "What is the structure of the mind?" but, "What is the function of the mind?" This new movement became known as functionalism. Truly American, the basic quest was to determine how the mind functioned. Encouraged by the work of

Charles Darwin, functionalism sought to discover how the mind functioned to aid human beings in their adaptation to their world. James's significant works included *The Principles of Psychology, Talks to Teachers* and *Varieties of Religious Experience.*

James is often credited with being the oldest and most influential American psychologist. Writing with the unusual clarity of a scientist, James opposed dividing consciousness into elements. Using a broader basis, James employed various methods in the study of conscious experience such as introspection, experimental methods, and comparative methods of study. James expressed the belief that there is no one exclusive method in the study of psychology.

James's followers made significant contributions to the growing field of functionalism. Granville Stanley Hall (1844-1924) achieved many firsts in American psychology, including: receiving the first American doctorate in psychology, entering as the first American student in the first year of the first psychology laboratory at Leipzig, developing the first scientific psychological laboratory in the United States, founding the first American journal of psychology, assuming the first presidency of Clark University, and becoming the first president of the American Psychological Association. Hall made additional contributions in the area of educational psychology. He was particularly interested in human and animal growth and development. Two of his famous works included *Adolescence* (1904) and *Senescence* (1922). Hall developed his recapitulation theory which states that each individual repeats in his own development the life history of his species.[11]

One of the early leaders in functionalism was John Dewey (1859-1952). Dewey wrote that behavior should be studied in the context of its significance to the organism in adapting to the environment. The proper study for psychology is the study of the total organism in its environment. Dewey believed that teaching should be oriented toward the student, not subject matter. Traditionally, schools in America, like those in Europe, had focused upon the acquiring of a body of information. Acquiring knowledge was the primary objective. Dewey advocated that education should seek to develop the individual by providing him opportunity to confront and utilize the subject matter. Learning by doing was synonymous with Dewey. Dewey proposed an experiment-based curriculum in the public-school system. His ideas became very popular in American education.

Two additional leaders in functionalism were James M. Cattell (1905-) and Edward L. Thorndike (1874-1949). Encouraged by Sir Francis Galton's study of individual differences, Cattell made significant contributions in the area of tests and measurements. Thorndike developed a view of learning that largely rested upon the importance of reinforcement. Thorndike developed three primary laws: the law of exercise, which states that bonds between stimulus and response are strengthened through repetition; the law of effect, which states that responses made prior to a satisfying state tend to be repeated; and the law of readiness, which states that if an animal is prepared to act, to do so is satisfying, and to be prevented from doing so is annoying.[12]

Behaviorism.—Ideas related to behaviorism appeared throughout the centuries. Ivan Pavlov (1849-1936) pioneered modern-day behaviorism. Pavlov, the son of a Russian clergyman, studied medicine. Rather than the clinical work of treating patients, Pavlov turned his attention to physiological research in the laboratory system. Pavlov's research involved the animal nervous and digestive systems. In his study of the digestive system of a dog, Pavlov made an important contribution that was to become known as classical conditioning.

In the laboratory setting, Pavlov noted that the presence of food would elicit salivation from the dog. The food would later be termed an unconditioned stimulus, and the salivation was a unconditioned response. Pavlov noticed that the sound of a buzzer when paired with the sight of the food eventually elicited salivation in the dog. After a number of trials, the buzzer eventually elicited salivation in the dog. The buzzer was the conditioned stimulus, and the salivation was a conditioned response. Classical conditioning became a cornerstone for describing learning and behavior.

In 1913 John Watson (1878-1958) in America published his behavioristic position entitled "Psychology as the Behaviorist Views It." Watson believed that no longer should psychology be concerned with speculation; rather, psychology must deal only with that which can be measured objectively, not with inner speculations. In the process, animal studies became the primary focus for understanding much of the workings of the human. Preoccupied with psychology being a true science, Watson proposed that the response of organisms is crucial. Watson's premise was that responses follow certain stimuli. If either the stimulus or the response is known, it is possible to predict the other. Much of psychological research applied to the field of learning reflects this basic behavioral perspective.

Watson proposed that all emotions are learned through classical conditioning. Watson conducted his "Baby Albert" experiments in which he classically conditioned an infant to be fearful of a white furry rat. Albert's fears of the white rat generalized to a number of other entities. Watson believed that given a dozen healthy infants, he could transform those infants into whatever he chose. Thus, Watson illustrated the importance of the environment in molding the life of the individual.

Watson's answer to the question of how humans learn was classical conditioning. The adult is the result of a series of childhood conditionings. While not developing a comprehensive theory of learning, Watson did believe in the importance of frequency and recency as primary factors in the learning process. Watson's position that "anyone could become anything" through environmental influences appealed to the American mind.[13]

The man who would continue this early work and would become synonymous with behaviorism is B. F. Skinner (1904-). Skinner proposed another type of conditioning, termed operant conditioning. In operant conditioning, the organism operates (acts upon) on its environment. In this process, the individual is more likely to continue the behavior if the behavior is reinforced. Nonreinforced behavior tends not to be repeated.

Skinner's proposal has had a tremendous significance in the scientific community. Much of present-day psychology is behavioristically based. The experiment and the laboratory became primary because science must concern itself with that which can be measured. Important applications have been made in the arena of education and behavior modification. Skinner has extended his belief from a laboratory setting to proposing a broad philosophical base for creating society. His book *Walden Two* illustrates this philosophy by describing a utopian society based upon principles of operant conditioning.

Gestalt Psychology.—Gestalt psychology developed in Germany through the work of three primary researchers: Max Wertheimer (1880-1943), Kurt Koffka (1886-1941), and Wolfgang Kohler (1887-1967). These theorists sought to focus upon the whole of experience, not the isolated parts of mental experience. The Gestalt psychologists explored how humanity perceives the whole. According to Gestaltists, meaning cannot exist without the context of the whole. Gestaltists hold that when sensory elements are combined, something new is formed. Perception extends beyond the basic physical data provided to the sense organs. Scientific investigation must focus on perception of the whole, not individual elements.

Kohler made significant contributions to learning theory through his study and work with apes and chimpanzees. In a series of experiments, Kohler developed the idea of insight learning in his book *The Mentality of Apes.* An insight refers to a spontaneous awareness of the relationship between the various elements in a situation. In his experiments, Kohler noted how his chimpanzees would suddenly gain understanding in how to solve a particular problem such as putting boxes together to form a stairway to reach bananas or putting two small rods together for the same purpose. Kohler argued that this observation was not the result of trial and error. Rather, the chimpanzee suddenly discovered a solution to the problem and tested this hypothesis.

One of the significant individuals who contributed to both Gestalt psychology and later the humanist movement was Kurt Lewin (1890-1947). Borrowing from the findings of Gestalt psychology, Lewin developed a "field theory" of learning which emphasizes the total perceived environment in its relationship to individual behavior and learning. To understand an individual and to work effectively with individuals in counseling or education, one must understand the concept of life space. Life space consists of the world as it relates to a particular individual. Life space is defined in light of the perceptions of the individual. Lewin would often diagram life space in light of goals or purposes. Life space fluctuates as goals and perceptions change.

Lewin held that a state of equilibrium exists between individuals and their environment. When the equilibrium is disturbed, a tension arises that leads to movement in an attempt to restore the equilibrium. Human behavior thus involves a continual appearance of equilibrium, disequilibrium, tension, movement, and reestablishment of equilibrium.[14]

Cognitive Theory.—Another researcher who made extensive use of animal studies was Edward Chace Tolman (1886-1959). Tolman developed the idea of cognitive maps which are mental representations of ideas, events, objects, or processes. In his work with rats in a puzzle maze, Tolman believed that the rats developed a mental picture of how to travel within the maze. When placed in the maze, the rat followed that cognitive map within itself. With increasing experience, cognitive maps are subject to further revision and development. Tolman believed that all animal behavior is capable of modification through experience.[15]

Biological Theories.—Recent advances in psychology and physiology provide a biological or neurological viewpoint of learning. One highly influential person is Donald Hebb (1904-), who developed a biological view of learning that centered around the neuron. Neurons work together in cell assemblies and phase sequences. Hebb believes that learning consists of the connections between neurons. Early stimulation in life provides a pattern of neurons from which all future learning develops. Stimulation is important as cell assemblies are activated and formed. These cell assemblies are the neurological explanations of how learning occurs.

The biological theories stress the chemical nature of the learning process. Two primary studies in this perspective are the study of rats and planaria. Studies with rats indicate that learning does change the basic brain chemistry. J. V. McConnell (1962) began experimenting by training planaria to turn in response to light. Trained planaria were then minced and fed to other planaria. Untrained planaria were prepared and fed to a second group of planaria. The planaria fed the "trained" food outperformed those that ate only the untrained planaria. Later experiments demonstrated that extracting RNA from trained planaria and injecting the RNA into untrained subjects had similar results. RNA memory transfer has also been performed with rats. However, not all studies have replicated such findings.[16]

Psychoanalytic School.—The psychoanalytic school of psychology, led by Sigmund Freud (1856-1939), presented a rather dismal view of humankind. According to Freud, human beings are biological creatures subject to their own inner turmoil. Basic personality structure is composed of three parts: the id, which represents the primitive human drives; the superego, which represents the values of morals developed from contact with family and society; and the ego, which seeks to mediate between demands of the superego and the demands of the id. Three levels of consciousness exist: the conscious of which humans are immediately aware, the preconscious of which humans can become aware with little effort, and the unconscious of which humans are unaware. According to Freud, much of human behavior is directly from unconscious levels.

Human life is motivated through two drives: the life instinct (*eros*) and the death instinct (*thanatos*). Human beings are in a constant battle between the life instinct and the death instinct. In addition, human behavior is largely unconscious, often from the unresolved conflicts of young childhood. These conflicts are too painful to deal with directly. Such painful conflicts are suppressed where they continue to direct human behavior. Unresolved conflicts often find expression in such manifestations as dreams, accidents, and Freudian slips.

Humanistic School.—The humanist school arose in particular reaction to the claims and advances made by the behaviorists and the psychoanalytics. The humanist school, led largely by Abraham Maslow (1908-70) and Carl Rogers (1902-   ), asserted that humans are much more than behaving animals and much more than mere victims of their own inner conflicts. Maslow described human beings' innate need to self-actualize their potential. He developed a hierarchy of needs which seeks to explain human behavior as an effort to satisfy unmet needs. Learning should consider human needs as primary motivational factors.

The emphasis on understanding an individual by understanding that individual's perceptions is a significant element of the humanistic view. Rogers has emphasized the importance of understanding the individual's world. Understanding the world as perceived by the individual is crucial to helping a person make needed changes. Like Maslow, Rogers emphasized that humans are motivated to reach their fullest potentials. Experiencing unconditional positive regard allows the person to reach that potential. Unconditional positive regard, that is genuine acceptance without meeting any conditions, creates the matrix from which growth and change can occur. Both Maslow and Rogers portrayed a much more positive view of humans as creatures capable of creative choice, working toward their own innermost potentials.

Social Learning Theory.—Social learning theory attempts to describe the process by which individuals acquire behaviors that are appropriate and inappropriate. In the 1940s Neal Miller (1909-) and John Dollard (1900-1980) proposed that imitation could be explained by basic principles of stimulus, reward, and reinforcement. Imitation is learned. Social learning can be explained through the general principles of learning.[17]

Another leading figure in social learning theory is Albert Bandura (1925-   ). Bandura's basic premise is that human behavior has cognitive, behavioral, and environmental factors. Working together, these factors form a reciprocal determinism. The degree of influence of each of these factors varies among situations as well as individuals. Bandura believes that human behavior is largely the result of a model rather than because of classical or operant conditioning.

Social learning can occur through the direct response consequences or through the observation of others. The behavior of another person, called a model, serves as an informational source. The individual then processes the information in order to perform the same behavior. Bandura distinguishes between learning and performance. Reinforcement plays a role in performance, not learning. Reinforcement includes extrinsic reinforcement, intrinsic reinforcement, vicarious reinforcement, and self-reinforcements.

Bandura holds that three behavior control systems interact in determining overall behavior. One group of behaviors is under stimulus control. These behaviors include reflexive acts (coughing, the startle reaction) and those responses learned through reinforcement. Outcome control includes those behaviors under control of consequences, not antecedent events or stimuli. Symbolic control involves those behaviors influenced by "mediation" or internal thought process.[18]

Learning Activity 4.2

1. Match the following with the BEST description.

_____ 1. Structuralism	a. focus on goodness of humans
_____ 2. Functionalism	b. interest in the basic unit of the mind
_____ 3. Behaviorism	c. focus upon the whole
_____ 4. Gestalt Psychology	d. concern only for the measurable
_____ 5. Humanistic Psychology	e. how does the mind work

2. Reaction and Response. Various theories of learning have been discussed. These theories include psychoanalytic, behaviorism, biological theories, cognitive theories, and humanistic theories. What is your reaction and response to each of these theories in light of Christian education? How are they compatible? Do they contain any elements that are incompatible with your understanding of Christian education? Explain.

SUMMARY OF MODERN LEARNING THEORIES

THEORY	LEADERSHIP	MAJOR IDEAS
Structuralism	Wilhelm Wundt	structural components of the mind
	E. B. Titchener	
Functionalism	William James	how the mind functions
	John Dewey	learning by doing
	Edward Thorndike	learning through reinforcement
Behaviorism	Ivan Pavlov	Classical Conditioning
	William James	Operant Conditioning
	B. F. Skinner	
Gestalt Psychology	Max Wertheimer	perception
	Kurt Koffka	whole of experience
	Wolfgang Kohler	Insight Learning
	Kurt Lewin	Field Theory
Cognitive Theory	E. C. Tolman	cognitive maps
Biological Theory	Donald Hebb	neurological basis for learning
Psychoanalytic	Sigmund Freud	life and death instincts
		early childhood experiences
Humanistic	Carl Rogers	individual perceptions
	Abraham Maslow	self concept
Social Learning	Neal Miller	observation
	John Dollard	imitation
	Albert Bandura	modeling

Figure 4.1

3. John Watson proposed that if given twelve healthy infants he could make of them what he desired. Do you think this idea has validity in light of Christian education? Why or why not?

Relationship Learning: Basic Premise

Each modern theory and theorist has significant insights for explaining the basic learning process, even as it applies to Christian learning. Each theory has its strengths and weaknesses. These theories fail to comprehend the full nature of humankind. While the theories may contain elements of truth and profound statements about human nature and the learning process, these insights are inadequate because they lack basic philosophical and theological assumptions. Because human beings are created in the image of God, humanity is set apart from the created order. Therefore, to understand the human race and to understand the process by which human beings learn, one must acknowledge those elements of human origin that can only be understood from the standpoint of humanity's Creator.

In developing a learning theory for Christian education, the individual must draw upon a multitude of sources, including learning theory, biblical foundations, historical, and philosophical sources. The remainder of this chapter is an attempt to provide an integrated understanding of the Christian learning process.

While volumes could be written to express the nature or essence of Christian learning, the basic premise is that Christian learning or Christian education is relationship learning. Various insights from secular theorists may be integrated where appropriate in explaining and fostering our relationship to the Creator. This relationship learning has primary influence in all the dimensions of an individual's life. Christian education should provide an opportunity for an individual to experience restored fellowship or relationship with God, self, others, and the created world. The end result of Christian education should be stewards who acknowledge their place of service, responsibility, and privilege in God's kingdom.

History reveals that the human race has an ever-continuing need for restored relationship. Before the Fall, human beings obeyed God. Out of this obedience, a perfect relationship flowered. Humanity lived in harmony with both animal and plant life; the man had a good relationship with his spouse; man and woman had a relationship with God in which they communed with Him. Humans have always had a basic need for relationship. After the Fall, human beings experienced a break in fellowship with God that resulted in a break in fellowship with themselves and the created world. Consequently, men and women have experienced a lifelong quest for relationships to fill the void in their lives.

This need for relationship expresses itself by numerous means throughout recorded history. Human beings have entered into various relationships with other humans, with institutions, and with themselves in light of their individual inclinations. In essence, humanity has sought to find a meaningful relationship.

Originally, humans worshiped the one true God. Later, humanity worshiped many gods. Consequently, the human race came under severe judgment for this lack of obedience. The judgment may flow from the various destructive nature of the relationships with other "gods." Regardless of the relationship, any relationship outside of the God-centered one will fail to achieve ultimate purpose and meaning. What God has created in human beings can only be realized in obedience to Him.

The biblical record portrays various attempts to find such meaningful relationships. After the flood, humanity attempted to build a tower to reach to the sky. All generations would praise the accomplishment of these tower builders. God intervened; the tower was never completed. At Sinai, God gave Moses the Ten Commandments, or Decalogue, to guide the behavior of the Chosen People. The Decalogue described the relationship between the human race and God and between human beings and their fellow humans.

History reveals that the Chosen People often failed to keep the laws and to be the priestly nation. New laws and regulations developed to help humanity keep the original Ten Commandments. These new regulations multiplied to the point that they became impossible to keep. Into this world of rules and regulations came Jesus. He sought to restore humanity's relationship to God. Hebrews 1:1-2 records, "In many and various ways God spoke of old to our fathers by the prophets; but in these last days he has spoken to us by a Son, whom he appointed the heir of all things, through whom also he created the world." Jesus' ministry reflects His obedience to the will of the Father.

In spite of various "wilderness" temptations and offered "shortcuts," Jesus did not seek a relationship other than obedience to the will of the Father. The powerful words uttered from the cross, "It is finished," carry eternal significance. Through belief in the Son of God, humankind no longer has to search for "meaningful" relationships. All human need is found in Christ Jesus. Subsequent relationships flow from this relationship with Christ.

Through the providence of God, we have a written account of the life and work of Christ Jesus and the early church. The Holy Scriptures provide us with what is sufficient for finding perfect relationship with God. Out of this relationship, human beings can experience restored relationships with themselves and the created order. Human beings can learn what it means to be the type of stewards God requires.

The written record necessitates the ability to read in order to understand the biblical message. In the course of time, the ability to read and the message of the Bible became restricted to a select few—the few highly trained clergy. The common person did not have access to the direct revelation of Scripture. What revelation was given was that which was transmitted by clergy. Often such revelation was colored with tradition, superstition, and ignorance.

A major turning point was the Protestant Reformation. Among its other benefits, the Reformation made it possible for each person to have access to the Scriptures. Leaders championed basic education so that people could read and understand the Word. Subsequent innovations in teaching sought to make the revelation understandable to various age groups. In the United States, the Sunday School movement was instrumental in providing basic education and a Bible for everyone.

Christian education concerns itself with a quest for the Word. In finding the Word, one finds the missing relationship with God, self, others, and the created world. Christian education helps persons find themselves fully aligned as God's stewards. Relationship to God must come first, and then relationships in these other areas will follow. Christian learning must seek to produce individuals who can discover the meaning of their own personal discipleship. Four basic domains of concern for Christian education are knowledge, understanding, attitude, and performance. Knowledge involves a beginning awareness of God's requirements. Understanding involves grasping more fully how our lives are to be lived in harmony with God's Commandments. Attitude involves developing an appreciation or outlook that reflects God's concern for the world. Performance involves acting in all of life based on truths and insights from the other domains.

These four domains provide areas of focus as Christian education seeks to lead in the restored areas of relationship: God, self, others, and the created order. Christian education helps individuals find fulfilled relationships "that they may have life, and have it abundantly" (John 10:10). The following represents the major ideas in a theory of Christian education.

Therapeutic Core

The central element of Christian learning involves a therapeutic core. If restored relationships are sought, it is appropriate that the beginning must be relational. One key ingredient in counseling and psychotherapy is the therapeutic context in which the counseling process will occur. One of the best illustrators of these elements is Carl Rogers. Rogers advocates the importance of the following three characteristics of an effective counseling relationship: congruence—being a genuine person who is growing, empathy—identifying emotionally with the individual, and unconditional positive regard—caring for the individual without qualification. Rogers points out that the client or counselee must perceive these qualities. The ability to communicate these qualities must be present. In addition, Rogers says that the relationship must be of some duration.[19] While Rogers and those practicing Rogerian counseling have experienced success with this approach, the question remains if this "working model" is appropriate for a biblical model of learning.

The "appropriateness" may be found in the life of Jesus. No one taught or loved better than the Son of God. While the words of Christ portrayed Truth, His loving compassion for humanity made it possible for the truth to be accepted. Jesus' teaching ministry began in active love and extended for a lengthy period. Jesus invested years in the equipping of a small number of disciples or learners. In genuineness, Jesus accepted others. Because Jesus began His teaching in the context of relationships, no better model exists.

A brief analysis of Rogers's three conditions may provide additional insight in establishing this therapeutic core in which Christian education operates. (See Figure 4.2).

1. *Congruence (Realness).*—Those involved in Christian teaching should be genuine Christians. The focus here is twofold: genuineness in their profession and demonstration of Christian faith and genuineness in themselves. Christian teachers should be real individuals in their humanity; Christian teachers should be real individuals in their Christian discipleship. Rather than denying strengths and weaknesses, these individuals should be genuinely growing in faith and service, even in struggles. Teachers should not put up facades; they need to be honest and genuine presentations of who they are. Only when we are honest with ourselves can we be honest with others. Congruence encourages others to find congruency in their own lives. Faithful lives encourage others to be faithful.

2. *Empathy.*—Empathy involves the ability to identify with the situations, feelings, and struggles of another individual. Serving as a bridge, empathy allows for contact between the teacher and the learner. Ultimately, empathy provides a basis for constructing lesson plans,

BRIDGE OF RELATIONSHIPS:
ALLOWS FOR CHRISTIAN LEARNING TO OCCUR

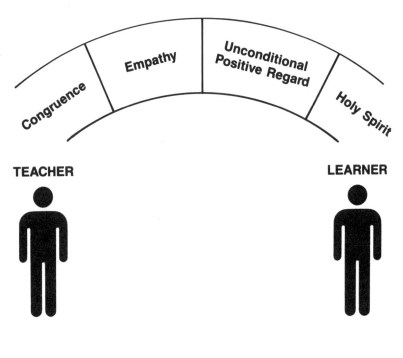

Figure 4.2

establishing curriculum patterns, and for guiding individual relationships. Empathy can be achieved in a variety of ways: reflecting that our own struggles, feelings, and questions are like those experienced by the learner; reading and studying the age group of the learner; expressing our own feelings with the learner; and prayerfully seeking to embody Christ's concern for each individual's potential.

3. *Unconditional Positive Regard.*—This characteristic involves accepting the individual without qualification. While it may not be possible to accept what an individual does, it is possible to accept the person in light of worth and potential. In the context of Christian education, individuals may find their first affirmation of acceptance based on who they are, rather than what they do. This quality is found in the life of Jesus. While not condoning individual sin and misbehavior, Jesus offered acceptance to all. Out of this receipt of acceptance, individuals discovered the ability to respond in needed growth and change. Reflecting upon our own acceptance by Christ, in spite of our shortcomings, may help us to accept others with their own.

4. *Holy Spirit.*—A fourth resource available to the Christian teacher is the Holy Spirit. The Holy Spirit is the primary resource that makes empathy, congruence, and unconditional positive regard possible. By providing new and renewed compassion and sensitivity, the Holy Spirit guides both the learner and teacher. The Christian teacher can develop significant relationships and insights through the power and prompting of the Holy Spirit. The distinctive therapeutic core in Christian education is established through the Holy Spirit.

Christian education is "something that is caught more than taught." This phrase becomes real through examining the quality of the life of the teacher in relationship to the learner. Out of feeling accepted, the learner is set on the course of finding proper relationships. The therapeutic core provides the bridge over which the learner can change cognitively, attitudinally, and in performance.

Learning Activity 4.3

1. Respond to the statement, "The therapeutic core (congruence, empathy, unconditional positive regard, and the Holy Spirit) is central to an understanding of Christian education." Have you ever been aware of such elements in a close teacher/disciple relationship in your life? If so, describe the process.
2. "Christian education is caught more than taught." What does this

statement mean?

Cognitive Structures

An important part of Christian learning theory involves the metaphor of the schema to describe the process of learning. The schema is a mental construct or image around which we gather information and through which we make responses. The schema allows a description of how information is processed in cognitive learning. For example, the young child possesses schemata which are basically reflex oriented. In early life we respond to our environment instinctively. Sucking is a basic instinct, and when something touches the baby's lips, the infant begins to suck.

As we mature, we respond to the world through our cognitive structures, or schemata. Such a response also applies to the Christian life. For example, children begin to develop their understanding of God from the world around them. If God is not worshiped in the home or the school, the cognitive structure develops in such a way that a response to God is marginal or nonexistent. Children begin to develop a rudimentary understanding of God by the manner in which their parents and teachers acquaint them with the Heavenly Father. A schema corresponding to God is established.

In an atmosphere where we pray, where Jesus is a friend, where we share our worship, and where we share our possessions with others, this type of cognitive structure develops within the growing child. It is crucial for the Christian parent and teacher to know God personally and to share this personal knowledge with others. We cannot help but teach; we cannot escape from influencing the formation of cognitive structures in others.

In addition to the schema, Jean Piaget introduced the concept of assimilation and accommodation which describes the basic processes by which we change cognitive structures and respond to our environment. Learning and performance involves assimilation and accommodation. Both processes should work in harmony to establish an equilibrium within the individual. Assimilation is the process by which we respond to objects and information in our environment in light of our already existing schemata.

An early example of assimilation can be seen when a child acquires language. The child develops the schema "doggie." The "doggie" schema represents all animals that remotely resemble the concept *dog*. In fact, the child will often respond to a wide variety of animals with the word *doggie*. New learning is done in light of previous learning. We learn the new in light of the old. Our future understandings of God will be performed initially in light of our previous understandings of God.

Accommodation is the process by which we change existing schemata to allow for new objects or information that does not "fit" the existing schemata. For example, the child may learn that a cat has unique characteristics that do not fit a part of the existing "doggie" schema. The assimilating child will refine the "doggie" schema and create a new "cat" schema. A young person may initially have a picture of God as only punishing. Through accommodation, the person may discover that God is also loving and kind. The schema for God is thus being modified to encompass more of the reality of God.

Piaget's metaphor provides a powerful mode for our understanding of what happens in the learning process and Christian growth. Initially, we may have our own schema of how God works. This schema may be accurate, inaccurate, or only partially accurate. As we grow and mature, our schemata will change; other schemata will develop as we experience new dimensions of His grace and love.

A cognitive view of Christian learning encourages the need for stimulation. A wide range of activities, including prayer, Bible study, and meditation promote Christian growth and development. In keeping with the Middle Ages' concept, "Nothing exists which did not first exist in the senses," the greater the variety of sensory stimulation, the greater the schema development. Various sources of stimulation are beneficial. Such stimulation may include the reading of Christian literature, mission trips, listening to Christian music, Christian testimonies, and active involvement in God's mission. If we are to hear God's voice, we must be in a place to be stimulated by His voice.

The metaphor of the schema, assimilation, and accommodation provide an insightful way of viewing Christian learning. Out of a therapeutic relationship, the individual develops schemata that foster Christian growth. In the process of growth and maturity, individual schemata undergoes change as assimilation and accommodation occur. No part of a Christian's pilgrimage is immune to new growth and understanding.

Learning Activity 4.4

1. Draw a diagram to illustrate the basic processes of assimilation and accommodation.
2. Think about an important part of your Christian life such as prayer, tithing, or attending church. Analyze how your ideas have changed over the years in your understanding of the practice. Describe any changes that have occurred in light of assimilation and accommodation. Be specific.
3. Imagination Analysis. Describe a hypothetical Christian who is exclusively an "assimilating" type in his daily life. What are his current activities and how do they change? Describe a hypothetical Christian who is exclusively an "accommodating" type in his daily life. What are his current activities and how do they change?
4. This chapter has described the term "schema." We all have schemata or concepts that are a part of our Christian value system. Look up the following verses in your Bible. Summarize what the verses mean to you (its schema). List five different activities that you can use to stimulate its growth and maturity in your life.

   1. John 3:16
      Basic Schema: _____
      Five activities to stimulate its growth and maturity in my life.
      a.
      b.
      c.
      d.

e.

2. Other verses include 1 Corinthians 6:19; Matthew 10:30-31; 1 Peter 3:12; Proverbs 2:6; Deuteronomy 8:18; Matthew 28:18-20; Amos 5:21-24; Romans 8:28-30; 1 John 4:7-12; and James 1:12.

Mature Confrontation

Basic to Christian learning is the necessity that the learning experience match the level of the learner. In addition, the learner should be encouraged to grow beyond the immediate level to a higher one. For this to be accomplished, the teacher must be aware of the present developmental level of the learner. Teachers may assess this level by talking with the learners about their lives, their needs, their goals, their problems, and their views of God. Following assessment, the subsequent learning experiences should challenge and stimulate a disequilibrium within the learner. This disequilibrium creates tension, and to restore equilibrium, the learner must resolve the tension.

Care must be exercised at this point. While there can be no genuine growth without some stretching or discomfort, the teacher must not abandon learners in their stressful growth experiences. Learners may be challenged and experience tension, but they may find no guidance in resolution. Consequently, they may abandon the schema totally or any attempt at resolution. In so doing, the learners may retreat to less mature forms of thinking and behavior.

The need for guidance in solving conflict is crucial. For example, an adolescent may begin to be challenged to think seriously about devoting a part of the week to God's service. To give new time to God may mean less time for previous personal pleasures. Adolescents may feel frustrated. They may want to be involved in ministry, but they may not want to relinquish their personal time. The Christian community must patiently help them in resolving their crisis. To leave them alone in painful frustration may lead to their abandoning the idea of serving God. In the future, they may be less likely to consider serving God again.

Too often we challenge the young mind and stop as the young mind

CHRISTIAN EDUCATION DOMAINS OF CONCERNS: RELATIONSHIPS BETWEEN THE DOMAINS

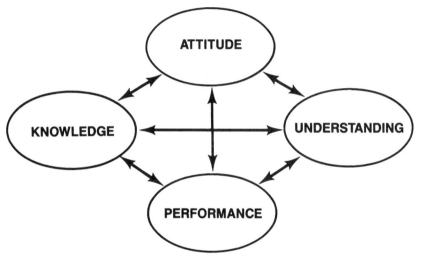

Figure 4.3

matures. How often do we continue the same learning experiences from year to year? What is challenging at one moment may not be challenging the next. How often do we do the same projects over and over? While the project may be worthwhile in itself, it may not stimulate the mental and spiritual growth necessary. Looking at the life of Paul, we see varied experiences that challenged and deepened his spiritual life. Christian education must provide those learning activities that promote and provoke growth and maturity.

Domains of Learning

Knowledge and Understanding Domains.—Knowledge, understanding, attitudinal, and performance domains are four areas of concern for Christian education. The interaction of the four will determine the living of the Christian life. (See Figure 4.3).

B. S. Bloom provided insights into the cognitive domain, involving both our knowledge and understanding domains. His six levels of cognitive development are: (1) knowledge—the ability to recall previously memorized material; (2) understanding—the ability to demonstrate the intended meaning of the material; (3) application—the ability to utilize information in novel ways in various situations; (4) analysis—the ability to decipher material into its related elements; (5) synthesis—the ability to bring various elements together in the creation of a new entity; and (6) evaluation—the ability to assess material in light of a given criteria.[20] The first level is typically called knowledge; the last five are known as understanding.

These six levels of Bloom's cognitive domain demonstrate the importance of increasing our knowledge beyond rote memory. Knowledge is more than being able to repeat the facts. Scripture and scriptural truth can be learned and relearned with increasing understanding and power. It is a mistake to assume that the individuals knows the material only when they can repeat the answer given to them. Maturing knowledge involves the development of understanding that leads to application. In this process, ownership of knowledge becomes stronger.

Developing knowledge may be facilitated by any number of educational principles. Selected principles include: providing experiences which actively involve the learner, involving as many senses as possible in the learning process, using advance organizers to help individuals prepare for what is to be presented, sharing the results immediately to give needed feedback, providing numerous and varied experiences for the learner, and providing new experiences for the individuals.[21]

Teaching for understanding, application, analysis, synthesis, and evaluation must also be developed. Guiding principles include: allowing learners to translate the ideas into new forms, showing how ideas relate to one another, providing opportunities for the learner to apply the information to new situations, helping the learner to learn how to break down information into its various parts, providing a systematic way of problem solving, helping the learner to create new products to illustrate the ideas, and helping the individuals to learn to assess situations based upon established standards.[22]

These levels of knowledge and understanding should be ever expanding in the maturing life. When there is no growth or development, life is arrested. When the individual fails to seek stimulating sources for growth or refuses to participate actively in the educational process, life is thwarted. The apostle Paul wrote, "When I was a child, I spoke like a child, I thought like a child, I reasoned like a child; when I became a man, I gave up childish ways" (1 Cor. 13:11). Regardless of how much we know, we can increase our understanding.

Attitudinal Domain.—Other sources often refer to this as the affective domain. The attitudinal domain incorporates the individual's mind-set and values. D. R. Krathwohl's affective domain provides insights into the attitudinal domain. Krathwohl's domain includes such ideas as the individual's reaction to subject matter, problems, or life experiences. Like Bloom's cognitive domain, Krathwohl's affective domain is divided from lowest to highest level. The first level, *receiving,* consists of the learner's demonstrating an initial awareness of an entity. The second level, *responding*, consists of the learner's becoming interested and minimally responding to the entity. The third level, *valuing,* consists of the learner's attachment or response to the entity because of perceived value. The fourth level, *organization,* involves the learner's transforming several values upon a situation. The fifth level, *characterization,* involves the learner's implementing a life-style that reflects a basic philosophy and commitment of life.[23]

The attitudinal domain or affective domain clearly reflects the individual's attitudes and values. The ultimate focus of Christian education is to conform to the image and nature of Christ. This does not occur automatically or instantaneously. Conscious effort and guidance are needed. Growth, like any other process, must be directed and nurtured. These levels of affective growth are particularly meaningful to Christian growth. For example, if having learners become committed Christian disciples is our goal, we must begin by having the learner become aware of the attractiveness of the Christian faith (receiving). One way of doing this may be through a caring relationship with the learner. Once we have gained the learner's attention, we have the opportunity to allow him or her to become more and more interested (responding). Gradually, the learner may experience the awareness of the value of the Christian message (valuing) with a degree of commitment. With growth and commitment, the learner may reach the levels of organization and characterization where the values learned become a part of the basic life-style and decision-making process.

Attitudinal or affective growth may be accomplished by keeping the following principles in mind: provide meaningful models, both live and symbolic, who represent the desired attitude; provide authoritative sources of the attitude; lead the learner to identify, specify, and understand the attitude; provide situations that may lead to meaningful emotional experiences; provide opportunities to practice the attitude; aid the learners in analyzing their own values and attitudes; and have learners dialogue concerning their insights.[24]

Performance Domain.—The performance domain involves putting into action what has been learned. The acquisition of motor skills or behaviors is demonstrated in the skill and performance opportunities using the skill. An analysis of E. J. Simpson's psychomotor domain may provide insight into areas of performance. This domain consists of the ability to perform physical acts with increasing skill and ease. Like other domains, Simpson's psychomotor domain is arranged in a hierarchy from lowest to highest. Briefly these levels include: (1) perception—the usage of sensory data to guide motor activity; (2) set—the readiness of the individual to perform some motor action; (3) guided response—the performing of a motor activity accompanied by instructor feedback; (4) complex overt response—the performing of behaviors involving complex movements; (5) adaptation—the performing of skills in which motor modification is made based upon situational demands; and (6) origination—the creating of original motor activities.[25]

Any number of principles may be stated regarding the performance of motor skills. Selected guidelines include the following: provide a general overview of the task to be performed or created, provide a step-by-step demonstration of the process, allow the learner to repeat the set of instructions for performing the task, provide guidance in the learner's initial attempts, provide repeated opportunities for performance with little or no guidance, and provide realistic conditions for practicing the task.[26]

Albert Bandura has provided additional insight into the performance domain. According to Bandura, learning and performance are not identical. We may learn information or acquire information. However, the learning may not be performed or demonstrated. The issue of reinforcement is significant to Bandura's understanding of learning and performance. Reinforcement promotes the demonstration of acquired learning. Environment influences both the degree to which learning will be achieved and the degree to which learning will be performed or demonstrated.

While the performance domain, especially in the area of motor skills, may appear to have little application to Christian education, there is application. Various activities or behaviors are a part of the Christian experience. Numerous church functions such as preaching, teaching, and witnessing involve motor skills or performance skills. The church should provide opportunities for people to acquire these skills. As they begin to put into practice what they have learned, many learners grow in their desire for more learning.

If Christian education concerns itself with preparing a person to live for God, the individual must be nurtured into performing that life in the best possible manner. All five domains influence and interact with each other. While we may target one area for a particular emphasis, all other areas are affected. Much like the workings of a kaleidoscope, a change in one area of learning produces changes in other areas.

Learning Activity 4.5

1. Respond to the statement, "Conflict is essential to growth." Once you have been involved in producing conflict in another individual, what is your response?
2. Challenge is a central part of growing in any discipline. What activities are you engaging in this year that are more challenging to your growth than the previous year or years? What activities would challenge you to grow in even more positive ways?
3. What is the difference between knowing and understanding? James wrote that even the demons believe and shudder (Jas. 2:19). How do demons' beliefs differ from a Christian's belief?
4. You may be a parent. If not, imagine that you are a parent for a moment. List some guidelines that you can follow to encourage or promote specific values or attitudes among your children.
5. List some specific activities that are necessary for the church to conduct its daily operations. How can you guide young Christians in conducting and feeling comfortable in these operations?

Gift Recognition

One of the most commonly overlooked aspects of Christian education may be the process of helping individuals discover and appropriate their various gifts. Immediately the question comes to mind: What is a gift? Does a *gift* have a supernatural or natural origin? Actually, both could be true. The gift may be a natural talent, ability, or individual difference. The gift may be a supernatural one, given for a special task. Just as God loves individually, Christian education must seek to maximize the individual gift potential of each.

Gifts find ultimate purpose in Christ's lordshp. They may be given at the time of rebirth or subsequent discipleship for the specific purpose of ministry. Whatever the point in time of acquiring the gift, the key is the recognition that it is ultimately given by God for God's purpose. Christian education should seek to discover individual giftedness that can be developed for God's ministry.

The New Testament discusses spiritual gifts in 1 Corinthians 12—14; Romans 12:3-8; Ephesians 4:1-8; and 1 Peter 4:7-11. Debate exists as to whether the New Testament gives an exhaustive account of the gifts or a representative account of the gifts. Walter Shurden in *The Doctrine of the Priesthood of the Believer* shares insights into these gifts: the common source of all gifts and the universal distribution of the gifts.[27] His work illustrates the wide diversity of the gifts and this diversity's significance for the church. This has application and significance for an understanding of the gifts of the church. Whatever gifts we possess, we possess them for ministry and service.

What would the church be like if we were all alike in the gifts, talents, and temperaments? Diversity is intended to allow for wholeness and completeness in the light of God's plan for human redemption. What would it be like if we were all an eye or all an ear? Because we are not, we need each other. Regardless of how gifted individuals might be, their giftedness is incomplete apart from the context of other gifted believers. The body needs the body. In so needing, we are reminded once again that we should not become too prideful of what we possess. Our talents or gifts may be wonderful; still they are inadequate if taken away from the context of God's purpose and God's people.

Church history illustrates how the understanding of spiritual gifts has been distorted. In the beginning, the disciples were believers who struggled and shared the ministry together. As "progress" was made, and centuries passed, the idea of ministry and giftedness was assigned to a special group we called the clergy. A division was created between the clergy and laypersons. The clergy possessed gifts; laypersons had none. During the Reformation, leaders like Luther returned to the idea that while some individuals receive a special call for a specific service, all Christians are called to ministry using their gifts.

Fortunately, God intends that each individual possess his or her own gift or gifts and exercise those gifts in the community of faith. The priesthood of all believers allows for the participation and exercise of gifts. One of the greatest gifts of the clergy is to enable other individuals to discover and appropriate their own gifts. These gifts are not for ministry in the narrow sense. Rather, the gifts are to be exercised in life; life itself is ministry.

Before leaving the issue of gifts, a few additional observations need to be made. The concept of *agape*—Christian self-sacrificing love— holds the gifts together. Many non-Christians possess gifts that are similar to the gifts possessed by those within the church. What is the difference? Have gifts illustrated in the Bible ever been used to destroy Christian fellowship rather than build Christian fellowship? Unfortunately, the answer is yes. The corrective answer may be love. Paul wrote: "If I speak in the tongues of men and of angels, but have not love, I am a noisy gong or a clanging cymbal" (1 Cor. 13:1). Love may be the key that separates and binds the gifts. A gift may acquire "spiritual" significance if it is directed toward the service of God and His people.

God has always developed individuals to carry His Gospel message in the context of their own generation. Those responsible for Christian education must assist those under their charge to ask the question: What gift do I have to share with my generation for God? The gifts assigned by God or needed by God may vary from generation to generation, but their purpose is to communicate God's redemptive message for both the individual and for the larger community.

How often have you looked at other individuals and wondered about their lives and their gifts? Have you ever pitied individuals because of their apparent lack of talent or worth? If so, we need to be reminded that all individuals are worthwhile because they are created in the image of God. All individuals are gifted. What is tragic is they may not have discovered their true worth or their own gifts. Talented individuals may show success in what they achieve. However, the ultimate success may not be reached if we have not discovered our giftedness in relationship to God's love and purpose.

Have you ever felt the pangs of jealousy about another person's gifts? Have you ever envied the gifts and recognitions given to another minister? One way to avoid this jealousy is to recognize and to utilize the gifts we ourselves possess. Our giftedness depends on God, on our own usage, and on the context of our sharing with other individuals. Creators we are not; created we are. As created life, our gifts belong to serving the Creator.

One focus of modern educational thought has been on the significance of the individual. The learner's individual differences are utmost in developing curriculum plans. However, this "modern" discovery has existed for centuries in light of gospel intent. In Christian growth, we each develop the giftedness within us. Christian learning seeks to find and develop the gift we each possess for service.

Learning Activity 4.6

1. What gifts do you possess? These may be spiritual or natural gifts. How do you know that you possess these gifts? How do you use these gifts?
2. Analyze your church, your Sunday School class, or any other Christian group to which you belong in light of spiritual gifts. Answer these specific questions.
   a. What various gifts are evident in your group?
   b. Who possesses which gifts?
   c. Do the gifts always work in harmony? Why or why not?
   d. How do you encourage gifts of the individual?
   e. Are there certain gifts that occur only as the group functions together?

Explain your answers.

3. Look at your immediate family or your extended family. Name each member by name and describe the giftedness of that person. How do you feel as you talk about the giftedness of your family members? What is your own giftedness? How do these gifts work together? How can these gifts work better together?
4. Who do you consider to be the most gifted individual that you personally know? How are the gifts used? Speak with the person about his or her gifts. How are these gifts developed?

Motivation

One of the central issues in any learning theory is motivation. What causes an individual to engage in learning and in performance? Simply stated, motivation is the "why" behind our behavior. Several sources of motivation exist. One primary form of motivation arises out of the therapeutic core. Because of being accepted and loved, the individual finds the motivational strength to grow, to learn, and to change. God's acceptance of us should motivate us to live for Him in keeping with His purpose. In the final analysis, motivation out of love is the most compelling. We live and learn because He loves us and sets us free.

A second source of motivation concerns basic human needs. As will be discussed in the following chapter, human beings have five basic relationship needs: physiological satisfaction, fellowship, knowledge, competency, and creativity. An individual's behavior is directed toward meeting these basic needs. A good motivational approach in Christian learning builds upon basic human needs. If there is a basic unmet need, attention should be directed toward fulfilling that need. The motivational source is internal: the needs of human beings and their own sense of gratitude at being accepted and loved.

The teacher can utilize this view of motivation in the learning process. For example, if there is a deficit in the person's need for fellowship, attention must be given to meeting those needs. If there is a specific broken relationship to God, self, or others, help must be specifically offered in finding solutions. Because humanity has a need for creativity, educational experiences should provide opportunities for creative expression. If an individual has deficit basic physiological needs, it is difficult to promote Christian growth until the deficit physiological needs are met. All of these needs continually influence human behavior. If Christian education can provide opportunities for growth, and these opportunities are perceived by the learner, individuals will seek such Christian education. Quality Christian education will not lack an audience.

Intergenerational Relationship

Basic to an understanding of the Christian education process is the idea of sharing the faith from one generation to the next. The next generation may be one of a different age or one of less faith maturity. One of the best ways of learning material and experiencing growth is to teach or to instruct another individual. When we teach material, we learn it. In order to teach we must first learn the material and then analyze it from all possible vantage points. In the process, the material becomes more and more our own. Both the teacher and the learner become learners. Each contributes to the growth of the other. While we "anew" the faith in others, we ourselves are "renewed" in our own faith.

Scripture clearly illustrates this partnership relationship in the life of Paul and Timothy. Timothy, a Greek, had the privilege of instruction under a godly mother, Lois, and a godly grandmother, Eunice. The relationship between Paul and Timothy afforded Paul an opportunity to share and train a Christian worker in an in-depth fashion; the relationship afforded Timothy an opportunity to learn the faith by watching a live model. When Paul was in prison and assessing his life, he wrote to Timothy and gave encouragement. The greatest gift that Timothy could give Paul would be to remain faithful to the gospel and to develop a relationship with another in discipleship.

Renewal occurs as we watch the birth and growth of faith in those we encounter. In Christian education, each generation has a legacy to convey to future generations. If one generation fails to teach another, the next generation may not experience the rebirth of faith. While each must discover and personalize the faith, each generation has the responsibility for communicating the faith.

Content, Methods, and Context

The basic content of relationship learning consists of the intersection of Scripture and the life concerns of the individual. Scripture teaches how human beings can find life and live life. Every aspect of human life and its relationship to scriptural truth is the basic material of which Christian education is made. Each Scripture teaching can be studied throughout the life span of the individual. As individuals grow and mature, their understanding of Scripture should grow correspondingly. For example, five-year-olds and sixty-five-year-olds can study God's love.

Any number of methods may be chosen for Christian education. The method chosen must not be one that undercuts the basic message of the gospel. For example, cruel nonredemptive criticism has no place in conveying the gospel of grace and love. Methods that discourage individuality are also highly questionable. Methodology must be congruent with the life needs of the learner. Lecture methods may be appropriate for the adult learner but inappropriate for the preschooler. Teachers must seek methods that involve the life and interests of the learner. Methods chosen must be consistent with Scripture, the needs of the learner, and the basic subject matter.

The context of Christian education is the context in which human beings experience their basic relationships. As will be discussed in a later chapter, three primary forms of Christian education exist: the family, the school, and the church. Christian education occurs wherever an individual confronts scriptural truth. Life itself is the basic content and context of Christian education.

Learning Activity 4.7

1. Can we determine the motivation of another individual? Can we be sure of our own motivation? What do you believe should be the motivation behind Christian education? Can you think of Scripture that supports your belief?
2. Imagine that you are teaching in a mission Vacation Bible School class for the first time. Your class is a group of young teens. How can you motivate the group toward the goals of school?
3. Have you ever had a special relationship with an older or more mature Christian, like that of Timothy and Paul? What specific insights in the Christian life did you gain from the older Christian?

Do you presently have such a relationship with a younger or less mature Christian? What values, if any, do you see in such a relationship?

4. Creative interpretation: think about the content, methods, and context of what you believe should be involved in Christian education. List these ideas on a sheet of paper. Now create a mural to depict these elements that you consider appropriate in Christian education.

5. What methods do you most enjoy in your own learning experiences? What methods do you most often use when you are teaching? What is the relationship? Do all people prefer the same teaching methods? If not, what is the ideal solution to the dilemma of method and individual preference?

Symbolization

Symbols are often regarded as red flags. Many of us fear that symbols denote something akin to graven images or idol worship. In some cases, symbols may reflect such graven images. However, we cannot escape the use of symbols and symbolic language. A part of our gift and privilege as human beings is the ability to create, utilize, and communicate with symbols. In fact, our high propensity for symbol usage separates us from the remaining created order.

Our language is symbolic. Our first sounds, words, phrases, and sentences are symbolic in nature. The Bible we cherish is symbolic in that the words represent the heavenly thoughts and instructions of our God. The words we choose to speak represent our attempts to communicate from our internal minds to the external world.

As humans we cannot escape the use of symbols. In fact, the symbols of our society communicate deep messages about ourselves. Look around your neighborhood. Our homes and apartments symbolize our need or value of having our own place of protection. We each tend to have our own form of transportation. The type and number of vehicles we have often suggests the type of priority we possess. Often our neighborhoods have places of worship. Our churches symbolize that we recognize the importance for worship beyond ourselves. Even the type of architecture—modern or traditional—suggests something about how we view ourselves and our approach to the community.

Symbolization can readily be seen on an individual level as well as a corporate level. Our clothing and where we buy it suggest an image we wish to project—how we wish to be perceived by others. Our society is often preoccupied with the "designer" label, whether it be certain initials or little animals. Where we invest our money or time is a good example of what schemata are important to us.

Not surprisingly, Christians should also examine the symbols they wish to employ. Rather than blindly using the symbols of others, which may or may not convey biblical truth, Christians should consciously choose their symbols. Choice and use of symbols is important. For many of us, our paychecks symbolize worth or productivity. Yet, how do we allocate or distribute our paycheck. Does the symbolic activity that flows from our paycheck reflect a God-centered approach to life? How do we allocate tithes and offerings? Is tithing first or last? Is it nonexistent? What we do with our financial resources suggests much about our nature and our values.

What about our worship services? What role does God play in them? What place does the Bible have in our church worship or educational services? Is Bible reading a central focus or a peripheral one? What about our church involvement? Are we actively involved in the ministry of the church? Is our concern more of being known or making Him known? What about the budget of the local church? Do we symbolically keep the vast majority of the income in the local area, or do we share that money with those around the world?

All we do symbolizes our beliefs and our priorities. What we do is important to God, to ourselves, and those around us. Scripture speaks of knowing them "by their fruits." In fact, a good measure of what we are is what we do. What we symbolize in our lives influences the lives of others. If we fail to demonstrate honesty, integrity, and caring for others or symbolize such virtues, it is not realistic to expect our children to automatically possess those qualities. Jesus became human and provided the best way for us to know God. By knowing Jesus we come to know the character and nature of God.

Rather than trying to avoid the issue of symbolizing, we must readily admit that we cannot escape symbolization. However, we can consciously choose the type of symbols that we will employ in our lives which convey the gospel message. Just as an initial or a "little animal" can represent the designer of a garment, we as Christians need to search for our own "Designer label." The "Designer label" involves what the Designer intended for us. No easy formula exists to determine what the symbols should be. In a sense, each must discover what is needed. Several principles may help in discovering those answers:

1. Symbols refer to words, ideas, philosophy, and objects as well as activities. A symbol is a broad term that denotes all in which we engage ourselves.

2. Symbols represent certain values. The source of symbols is some type of value system. As we choose, we must consider the values that underlie the symbols.

3. Symbols must not be misunderstood in terms of meaning. A temptation exists to confuse the symbol (form) with its meaning (essence). We may often conduct the symbols or go through the motions of habit and miss the intended meaning.

4. Each generation must formulate its own symbols. While we may continue to use the symbols of another generation, each generation must struggle with the meaning of what it means to be Christian. Once this is decided, choice of symbols becomes more meaningful with less possibility of losing the meaning.

5. Symbols must be chosen in such a way as to foster proper relationship not only with God, but with self and others.

6. Choosing symbols must be done out of a relationship of obedience to God. Christian education deals with the ultimate human destiny. Ways of promoting proper relationship must be done with careful thought.

7. Symbols must be developed in the context of both the individual as well as the community. What we do personally, as well as corpo-

rately, must be viewed with equal passion and dedication.

8. Symbols teach the world of our relationship to ourselves, to others, and to God. We need consistency in our symbol usage. For example, we cannot profess love with words and then exploit with other behaviors. Consistency in symbols is essential.

In summary, Christian education will employ symbols or symbolic activity. We cannot escape symbols that express our understanding of God and humanity. In whatever we do, we are symbolizing. Christian education must carefully analyze its practices (symbols) to ensure credibility with the gospel.

Learning Activity 4.8

1. Look around your house, your apartment, or your dormitory room (whatever you consider home). What objects or symbols are especially significant to you? What do these objects or symbols represent?
2. If you could "save" only three objects from your home, what objects would these be? What does your selection say about you?
3. What symbols or symbolic activity does your church engage in during a typical week? What do these objects or symbols represent? What is the intended meaning behind each activity?
4. If a visitor from a foreign country were to visit your home church and examine your church bulletin, what would he or she discover is significant to your congregation?
5. Look at your church budget. What is symbolized by the budget? Do you like or dislike what it represents? Explain.
6. What symbols do you believe would help teach or instruct the world that you are a Christian disciple?
7. Imagine that you are in charge of a time capsule to be opened in one hundred years. You are responsible for placing objects in the time capsule that represent what your church and you consider important expressions of Christianity. What would those objects be? Why?

Integration

This element of Christian education is important on several levels. First, individuals, as they grow in the knowledge of Jesus Christ, must learn to integrate that knowledge in terms of their daily living. A problem that we often encounter in terms of "religious" individuals is the manner in which individuals divorce their "religion" from the other aspects of their lives. In fact, this pattern often reveals itself in Scripture. Individuals will often profess with their mouths loyalty and worship of God and then deny that worship through their exploitation of others. Knowledge in Christ must extend to all areas of life, with proper integration and value reflection. If not, we have a compartmentalized faith which may not be a maturing faith.

In addition, those involved in the educational process must seek various ways to integrate the faith with the life concerns of the individual. For example, the various individual developmental concerns must be addressed and related to biblical teachings. If not integrated, the biblical teachings may be abandoned; the individual may seek other philosophies or other false gods that do address basic developmental needs.

Individuals must learn to integrate what they know biblically with what they are discovering in secular learning. All truth is God's truth. With increasing cognitive growth and experience, the individual will be confronted with challenging questions. As one becomes more intellectually enlightened, one may abandon the faith. Christian education must meet the challenge of secular learning. Mature minds need mature teaching.

This type of integration is important when the individual confronts other disciplines of knowledge that challenge one's basic understanding of Christianity. Integration enables the Christian to confront, to challenge, and to witness to the academic and the technological world. The command to go into all the world and make disciples may be applied to go into all arenas of knowledge and bring new disciplines into their proper relationship to God.

Outcome

The basic outcome of relationship learning is producing Christian stewards who utilize their giftedness in relationship to God, self, others, and the world. Each of these relationship directions has a cognitive, attitudinal, and performance element. Christian education should seek to help the individual in each of these relationships. We are created for fellowship and must live lives in fellowship with and in praise of the Creator.

Learning Activity 4.9

1. Do you feel that God has called you to be involved in integrating His truth with any specific areas of life? If so, what areas of life should be your focus of attention? How can you be involved in integrating the faith into your daily life?
2. What do you believe should be the outcome of the Christian education process? Support your answer with specific examples or Scripture references.

Notes

1. Leahey, 40.
2. Ibid., 47-52.
3. Daniel N. Robinson, *An Intellectual History of Psychology* (Madison: The University of Wisconsin Press, 1986), 120-32.
4. Leahey, 61.
5. Ibid., 71-76.
6. Robinson, 152-54.
7. Duane Schultz and Sydney Ellen Schultz, *A History of Modern Psychology*, 4th ed. (New York: Harcourt Brace Jovanovich, 1987), 21-28.
8. Ibid., 28-37.
9. Leahey, 143-44, 168-69, 279-80.
10. Schultz, 40-42.
11. Schultz, 141-46.
12. Guy R. Lefrancois, *Psychological Theories and Human Learning*, 2d ed. (Monterey, Calif.: Brooks-Cole Publishing Co., 1982), 36-40.
13. Schultz, 195-201, 208-19.
14. Lefrancois, 141-54.
15. Schultz, 229-34.
16. Lefrancois, 250-52.

17. Kay Deaux and Lawrence S. Wrightsman, *Social Psychology in the 80s*, 4th ed. (Monterey, Calif.: Brooks-Cole Publishing, 1984), 16-17.

18. Lefrancois, 286-89.

19. Jess Feist, *Theories of Personality* (New York: Holt, Rinehart and Winston, 1985), 420-24.

20. See B. S. Bloom, et al., *Taxonomy of Educational Objectives: Handbook I, Cognitive Domain* (New York: D. McKay, 1956).

21. LeRoy Ford, *Design for Teaching and Training: A Self-Study Guide to Lesson Planning* (Nashville: Broadman Press, 1978), 118.

22. Ibid., 163, 195.

23. See D. R. Krathwohl, et al., *Taxonomy of Educational Objectives: Handbook II, Affective Domain* (New York: D. McKay, 1964).

24. Ford, 225, 242.

25. See E. J. Simpson, "The Classification of Educational Objectives in the Psychomotor Domain," *The Psychomotor Domain*, vol. 3 (Washington, D.C.: Gryphon House, 1972).

26. Ford, 292.

27. Walter Shurden, *The Doctrine of the Priesthood of the Believer* (Nashville: Convention Press, 1987).

5

Learner Characteristics and Faith Development Across the Life Span

An Overview of the Relationship Theme

Faith development cannot be separated from the various age-level characteristics and development of the individual. Insights from cognitive development, moral development, and social development influence the religious growth and its accompanying Christian educational practices. While findings from religious or faith development are presented, major focus is given to a relationship view of personality and faith development.

Human personality consists of four components: sensate (physical), intellect, emotion, and will. These four elements exist on both a conscious and an unconscious level. Each person has varying strengths and weaknesses in each of these areas. Human behavior is a result of both heredity and environment, and is directed by meeting unmet needs (the result of both hereditary dispositions and environmental influences). These needs include physiological satisfaction, fellowship, knowledge, competence, and creativity. They are traced through various age levels from the prenatal period to death, along with selected developmental characteristics. Understanding these characteristics and needs provides guidance in seeking to develop Christian education across the life span.

Various models have been formulated to describe the developmental processes. Each approach has its own strengths, weaknesses, contributions, and limitations. Some approaches have direct implication for understanding the religious development of the individual. Select-

ed approaches will be presented which have this religious development implication. Following the findings of these theorists, personality development and its implications for life span Christian education
will be presented.

Cognitive Development

Cognitive development involves age-related changes occurring in
mental activity. Included in this mental activity are thoughts, memories, perceptions, attentions, and language. One of the chief researchers in cognitive development was Jean Piaget (1896-1980). Piaget's
contributions of schema, assimilation, and accommodation have been
discussed in the previous chapter.

Piaget identified four stages of cognitive growth and development:
the Sensorimotor Period, the Preoperational Period, the Concrete Operational Period, and the Formal Operational Period. The Sensorimotor Period (birth to two years) involves learning coordination between
sensations and motor movements. Beginning with the child's reflex
ability, this period ends with the child's use of primitive sentences.
The Preoperational Period (two to seven years) involves the increased
use of language and symbolic thought. Thinking during this period is
primarily egocentric.

The Concrete Operational Period (seven to eleven years) involves
the increased use of logical thinking that employs concrete objects.
Gradually, the child acquires the various phases of the principle of
conservation. The last stage of cognitive development is known as the
Formal Operational Period (eleven to the adult years). In this last
phase, mental operations are carried out in symbolic form. The individual is capable of moving beyond concrete experiences to the formulation and testing of various abstract hypotheses. In each of these
phases, Piaget sought to describe the way in which the child thinks.

The thinking processes of children are qualitatively different from
those of adults. Amusing answers children give reflect how children
actually think and view their world. In seeking to communicate with
children, it is important to understand their thought processes. How a

child processes information affects the practice of Christian education. Further discussion of Piaget's findings will be given later in the chapter.

Moral Development

Moral development involves the processes by which an individual governs one's behavior in relationship to other individuals. Based upon cognitive research, Piaget made significant contributions to our understanding of moral development. Piaget believed two modes of moral thought exist. The first mode, called moral realism, is associated with children from four to seven years. The moral realist has three central characteristic concerns: (1) rightness or goodness is based upon the consequences of the behavior; (2) rules are viewed as all powerful and unchangeable; and (3) the belief in imminent justice is held. The second mode, called moral autonomy, is associated with children ten years and older. The moral autonomist has three central characteristic concerns: (1) the rightness or goodness of the behavior is based upon the intentions of the individual; (2) rules are viewed as socially agreed upon conventions, subject to change; and (3) the belief that punishment is not always inevitable.[1]

Elaborating upon Piaget's work, Lawrence Kohlberg (1927-   ) developed three levels of moral reasoning. Each level is divided into two substages. Level I, or the Preconventional Level, involves the punishment or reward orientation. Moral decisions are based upon the desire to obtain rewards or avoid punishment. Level II, or the Conventional Level, involves a societal orientation. Moral decisions are based upon the desire to be regarded as a good member of society or to keep the society functioning. Level III, or the Postconventional Level, involves a higher orientation beyond social or societal conventions. Moral decisions are based upon concern for the benefits of society or concern for higher ethical principles. Kohlberg's levels focus on the process of thinking beyond the behavior, not the behavior itself.[2]

One aspect of the Christian faith involves the ability to make decisions based upon an understanding of God's Word and leadership.

Scripture teaches that not only are decisions or behaviors important, but attitudes are significant. Two people can engage in the same act and yet have different motives or motivations. Research in moral development may assist in discovering the motivations for our own behavior, even as it applies to the Christian faith.[3]

Social Development

Social development involves an individual's interactions with others in a social context. One highly influential theorist in the area of social development is Erik Erikson (1902-) and his work with the psychosocial stages of man. According to Erikson, each stage in life builds upon or develops from a previous stage. This idea is known as the epigenetic principle. Each stage develops around a crisis event in the maturing life (psyche) of individuals in their environment (social world). The degree to which one resolves each of the conflicts impacts the next stage and consequent behavior.

Stage one, *trust versus mistrust,* corresponds with birth to approximately two years. In this stage, the individual faces the crisis of trusting or mistrusting one's environment. The degree of resolution of the conflict becomes a part of the individual's growing ego. Stage two, *autonomy versus shame or doubt,* corresponds approximately with two to three years. In this stage, the individual faces the quest of experiencing independence from one's environment. Feeling confident about one's ability leads to the development of autonomy; feeling a lack of control or ability leads to the development of shame or doubt.

Stage three, *initiative versus guilt,* corresponds approximately with three to five years. In this crisis, the child may experience a sense of power in which initiative is achieved. Should children be dominated by their environment and feel powerless, they may develop guilt. Stage four, *industry versus inferiority,* corresponds approximately with the elementary school years, six to eleven. Mastery of basic skills allows for the development of industry; failure to master basic skills allows for the development of guilt. Stage five, *identity versus role confusion,* corresponds approximately with the adolescent years, twelve to nineteen. In this crisis, individuals seek to discover their identity and their identity with their cultural group. Discovering who one is leads to identity; failing to discover who one is leads to role confusion.

Stage six, *intimacy versus isolation,* corresponds approximately with the young adult years. In this stage, the individual must learn to establish meaningful relationships with others or to remain isolated. Stage seven, *generativity versus stagnation,* corresponds approximately with the middle adult years. Here, the individual must confront the issue of becoming involved in caring for the next generation (generativity) or remaining preoccupied with self (stagnation). Stage eight, *ego integrity versus despair,* corresponds approximately with late adulthood. In this crisis, a person reviews the course of his life. If a general feeling of satisfaction is achieved, an individual acquires ego identity; a general dissatisfaction leads to ego despair.[4]

Learning Activity 5.1

1. Create a series of cartoons to depict how we grow in our cognitive ability.
2. Paraphrase Kohlberg's three levels of moral reasoning. Create examples to illustrate how these levels might operate in the life of a Christian.
3. Fill-in-the-Blank. Fill in the blank with the appropriate term.
   Erikson's Psychosocial Stages of Development
   a. Trust versus _____. (Birth to two years.)
   b. _____ versus Shame or Doubt. (Two to three years.)
   c. Initiative versus _____. (Three to five years.)
   d. _____ versus Inferiority. (Six to eleven years.)
   e. Identity versus _____ Confusion. (Adolescent years.)
   f. Intimacy versus _____. (Young adult years.)
   g. _____ versus Stagnation. (Middle adult years.)
   h. Ego _____ versus _____. (Older adult years.)

Religious Development

One of the earliest writers to portray the spiritual pilgrimage of the individual was Augustine of Hippo (354-430). His work *The Confessions* reveals an autobiographical understanding of religious experiences. Another early writer, Bernard of Clairvaux (1090-1153) wrote *On the Love of God* in which he described four progressive views of life. Each of these views or levels revolves around the theme of love. Stage one involves a self-centered type of love. Stage two includes a love for God based upon self needs. Stage three involves a love for God based upon God's sake. Stage four includes a love for self based upon God's sake. In Bernard's approach, religious growth incorporates the dynamic growth process of love.

John Bunyan (1628-88) in *Pilgrim's Progress* depicted ten stages of the Christian pilgrimage from the City of Destruction to the Celestial City. Soren Kierkegaard (1813-55) depicted three stages of life: the aesthetic, the ethical, and the religious. The aesthetic life seeks the satisfaction of the senses; the ethical life seeks one's duty, and the religious life emphasizes life before God. Kierkegaard sought to provide a qualitative understanding of the self actualizing its potentialities; he provides both vertical and horizontal interpretations of relationships in achieving selfhood.[5]

One modern theorist who has explored the religious growth of the individual is James W. Fowler. Fowler describes stages in which the individual develops meaningful world views. Fowler's concern is the actual process of faith development. Stage zero or a prestage level, known as Primal or Undifferentiated Faith, involves the very young child. Here the young child is highly influenced by the quality of care that is given. Stage one, known as *Intuitive-Projective Faith,* corresponds approximately with three to seven years. Highly egocentric, the child cannot distinguish between fantasy and fact. Here the child is influenced by the example, actions, and stories of significant adults. Stage two, known as *Mythical-Literal Faith,* corresponds approximately with seven to eleven years. The child assumes the symbols of the environment in a literal fashion. Conflicts or contradictions in stories told lead to a reflection of meaning.

Stage three, termed *Synthetic-Conventional Faith,* corresponds roughly with adolescence. Some individuals may not proceed beyond this level. Here the individuals begin to structure their world in light of interpersonal terms. Although not examining its significance, the individuals develop an ideology upon which their lives revolve. Stage four, called *Individuative-Reflective Faith,* roughly emerges at college age or young adulthood. Here individuals begin to assume responsibility for their own life commitments. This stage involves the examination of symbols in light of conceptual meanings. Stage five, known as *Conjunctive Faith,* involves the recognition of truths in one's own faith and the faith of other individuals. Individuals continue to work for their own faith and its symbols; however, they are aware of its limitations. Stage six, known as *Universalizing Faith,* is rare. These individuals identify with a type of universal brotherhood and work enthusiastically toward that end.[6]

Learning Activity 5.2

1. List key words that you feel are significant in a discussion of Christian growth and development.
2. A young mother asks you, "Why are people different, even Christians?" What is your response?
3. Create a time line of your life. Include significant dates, places, and people to your Christian pilgrimage. Based upon your time line, summarize your Christian growth and development.

A Summary Overview of Relationship Personality

In order to understand the relationship concept of Christian education, it is crucial to understand a basic view of personality growth and development. Basic to this understanding of personality development is a biblical approach to life. Human beings were created in the "image of God" for fellowship and relationship. Prior to the Fall, human beings had perfect, harmonious relationships with God, others, self, and created order. After the Fall, humanity experienced broken relationships in all areas. (See Figures 5.1 and 5.2).

Human personality consists of four components: sensate (physical), intellect, emotion, and will—all established in perfect harmony. After the Fall, these four elements became unbalanced. Today, each individual may possess strengths or weaknesses in any of these areas. Prior to the Fall, these four elements existed on a conscious level. After the Fall, they came to exist on various levels of consciousness and unconsciousness.

Out of this Fall experience, certain needs emerged that direct human behavior. These needs center around the concept of relationship: need for physiological satisfaction, need for fellowship, need for knowledge, need for competency, and the need for creativity. Each individual differs in the degree of these needs. The most basic are: the need for physiological satisfaction and the need for fellowship. They provide the basis for the satisfaction of other needs. The remaining needs are not arranged in a hierarchical fashion. Rather, the needs for knowledge, competency, and creativity are sought simultaneously. Each has various levels and strengths. A deprivation of any need creates a drive that seeks to satisfy the need. (See Figure 5.3).

A person is a product of the complex interaction of heredity (individual differences, relationship needs, structures of personality) and environment (the total context of relationships in which we live). Each family or cultural group provides the basic framework for the manner in which these basic needs find expression. Certain cultures tend to produce certain personality types, as do families. For example, certain families tend to produce lawyers, doctors, teachers, or missionaries. Other families may produce relationships where child abuse and family violence appear in each generation. Whatever an individual becomes is a complex result of biological differences, private choices, and environment. Each individual seeks to fulfill these basic relationship needs.

People pass through various phases or stages as they develop. While not possessing exclusive determinism, each stage does influence the

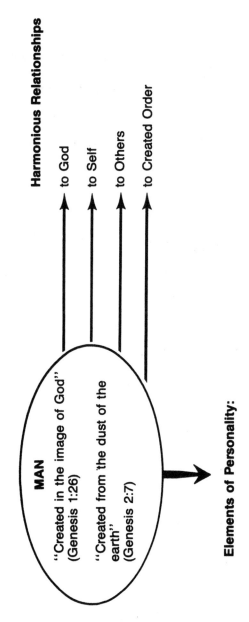

BEFORE THE FALL

Harmonious Relationships

to God

to Self

to Others

to Created Order

MAN

"Created in the image of God" (Genesis 1:26)

"Created from the dust of the earth" (Genesis 2:7)

Elements of Personality:

Balanced; Conscious Levels

Sensate (Physical)

Intellect

Emotion

Will

Figure 5.1

AFTER THE FALL

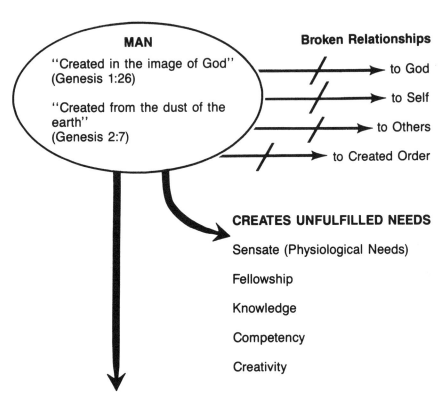

Figure 5.2

LIFE DEVELOPMENT

Man's Behavior

(Result of seeking to meet needs)

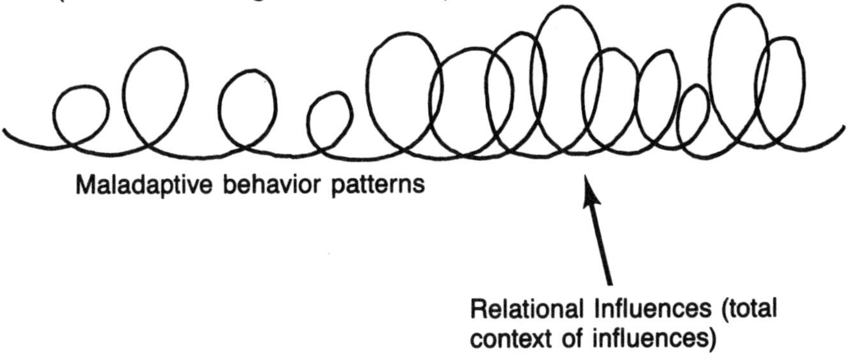

Maladaptive behavior patterns

Relational Influences (total context of influences)

Behavior patterns may lead *away* from or *to* God.

Figure 5.3

next stage of life. The basic relationship needs seek expression and direct behavior throughout the life span. Each need may have greater strength or potency during selected life phases. In this growth process, life behavioral patterns may develop that are either adaptive or maladaptive. These patterns are highly influenced by other individuals, social, and cultural experiences in which the individual comes into contact. Based upon experience and choice, human beings, throughout their lives, may experience ever-increasing maladaptive or adaptive patterns. Humans have the capacity to progress in adaptive patterns or to regress in maladaptive patterns in seeking to meet these relationship needs.

At any point in life, Christian conversion brought about by the work of the Holy Spirit and the individual's consent can occur. Con-

CHRISTIAN CONVERSION AND CHRISTIAN GROWTH

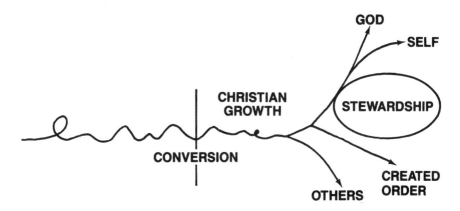

**RESTORING BALANCE OF PERSONALITY:
RESTORING RELATIONSHIPS TO GOD, SELF,
OTHERS, AND CREATED ORDER**

Figure 5.4

version begins to bring about the restoration of relationship identity (maturing harmony of the sensate, intellect, emotion, and will aspects of personality). From this viewpoint, the maladaptive behavioral patterns begin to become more adaptive as the individual moves toward God. The individual comes to possess the Mind of Christ. This new mind renews and directs behavior toward God's service. (See Figure 5.4).

No two individuals will grow in the same precise manner. The environment in which we live will influence our Christian growth. Certain environments promote more Christian behavior than other environments. In addition, each individual grows in accordance with a willingness to be conformed to the image and purposes of Christ through the work of the Holy Spirit.

The result of growth is the slow maturation that produces a steward of God who seeks to bring honor to God by a life of service to the Creator and one's fellow human beings. While each life is different, one common indicator of growth and commonality with others is the mark of *agape* love—self-sacrificing love. This love can only occur as relationship has been established with Christ, Who is Love Incarnate.

Life Characteristics and Faith Development

Faith development is a lifelong quest for both learner and teacher. In understanding how Christian faith develops and is nurtured, it is crucial to understand the various characteristics and needs of the learner throughout the life span.

Prenatal Development

Developmental changes transform the human zygote into a human being capable of marvelous learning and accomplishment. Numerous publications stress the need for parents to stimulate their child educationally from the crib and even prenatally. The parent is often confused with what should be expected from the young child. How much learning can an infant accomplish? Research indicates that learning occurs not only at birth but also in prenatal development. Studies show that an individual can learn—if learning refers to a change in behavior brought about by environmental stimuli—while inside the womb.[7] Because of the importance of heredity and environment, the prenatal period is influential in the unborn's future growth and development.

Various teratogens (damaging agents) can influence prenatal development and cause birth defects. Such teratogens include poor nutrition, social drugs, prescription drugs, radiation, and x-rays. Each of these can have impact upon the growth and development of the newborn. The degree of impact depends upon the age of the unborn, its own inherited predispositions, the severity of the teratogen, the combination of other teratogens, and the length of exposure. Results of these teratogens vary greatly. For example, an unborn child exposed to rubella during the first trimester can experience damage to the central nervous system resulting in brain damage, deafness, and blindness. Cigarette smoking can produce premature births, lower birth weights, and less alert newborns. Additionally, stress can influence the growth of the unborn. Such factors include stress regarding an unwanted pregnancy, concern over limited financial resources, stress over the anticipated changes associated with new life, the father's emotional health, and its impact upon the newborn.

While teratogens can negatively impact the health of the child, focus should be placed on those factors that positively influence the life of the child. The church can provide many ways of meeting the developmental needs at this stage of life. Encouragement and reassurance to the parents will have a direct effect on the child. The Hebrews considered the birth of a child to be of high priority. The church today can place a high priority on the life of the unborn by placing high priority and importance on the family as they anticipate the birth of the child. Helping to provide for the best prenatal environment will encourage the healthy growth of the future elements of personality (sensate, emotions, will, and intellect).

Such emphasis could involve workshops and training sessions on various aspects of the new parent's life including financial management, baby care information, communication, and adjusting to a new life in the household. The church can join in the celebration of the new life and become a community which nurtures that child toward a mature and fulfilled life in the Christian community by both birth and rebirth. As Luther indicated, Christians should be aware of the serious nature of the bringing of children into the world. Children have an innate right to be trained. The church has a Christlike responsibility to be involved in that training.

Learning Activity 5.3

1. What do you consider to be the structure of human personality? Explain.
2. How did humanity change after the Fall? What is the significance

of the Fall for today's life?

3. What are the differences between the Christian life and the non-Christian life? What are any similarities?

4. The text describes five basic human needs (sensate, relationship, knowledge, competency, and creativity). Do you agree or disagree with this list? Describe your reactions. What modifications, if any, would you make?

Infancy

Infancy covers the birth of the child until the end of the first two years of life. This period describes the time when the child is totally dependent upon the world for its existence to the time when the child becomes a more independent personality. The foundations for personality are laid during these early years of life. Initially, the major focus of growth is upon meeting the sensate or the physiological needs.

The child begins life with actions that are largely involuntary. His movements are like those carried on in the womb. Throughout the first two years, the child achieves more voluntary muscle control. The infant begins life with a cry. By the end of the second year, the child is learning to think and to communicate through symbols—language. The ability to use language will revolutionize a child's life and will impact basic needs of relationship, knowledge, competency, creativity, and physiological satisfaction.

Differences in a child's personality can be traced to the early stages of life. Babies are not all alike. While they may have somewhat similar appearances at birth, babies soon develop their own set of characteristics that distinguish them from other babies. Such characteristics include: sociability, activity level, irritability/soothability, rhythmicity, adaptability, intensity of reaction, distractibility, attention span and persistency, threshold of responsiveness, and mood quality. While these qualities can be noticed at birth, they are not firmly embedded.[8] These characteristics can be modified through environmental influences. Often adults are quite different from characteristics displayed in infancy.

What can the church offer in specific ways to the child at this age? Insight can be found in the work of Erik Erikson. Erikson believes that during the first two years of life, the child learns to trust or to mistrust the world. The answer to that question will be determined by how the child perceives the world in relationship to his basic needs over which he has no control. Will there be adequate nutrition? Will there be a change of diaper when needed? Will there be warmth from the cold? The manner in which basic needs are met will establish the way the child acts and reacts to the world.

Satisfaction of the needs for relationship, physiological satisfaction, and stimulation are crucial to development. Infants that do not receive warmth or emotional stimulation have been reported to experience thwarted growth. In severe cases, the child may die. Maternal deprivation syndrome has been used to describe the phenomenon that occurs when a child gives up the will to live and dies because of a lack of warmth and stimulation.

One of the most significant developmental milestones occurs during infancy. This milestone involves bonding, or forming warm attachments (relationships), between the child and adults. Bonding is extremely important for the formation of later development and later relationships. Bonding occurs between the child and the primary caregiver, usually the mother.

This bonding or attachment occurs in phases. In the first four to six months, the child tends to have nondiscriminating attachments to adults. In the following months, the child tends to develop a positive attachment toward one or more caregivers. This primary attachment may last from one year to eighteen months. Fear of strangers and separation anxiety appear to develop one to four months after primary attachment has been formed. In separation anxiety, the child becomes visibly upset when away from the primary caregiver. By approximately eighteen months, separation anxiety disappears.[9]

Ministry to the child will largely be accomplished through ministering to the parents and other family members. In both the home and the church, the child needs to find a trusting place and trusting, con-

sistent adults. The church's responsibility to the child is through nurturing the parents in providing warmth, security, and trust. With increasing numbers of two-income and single-mother families, the
church may find a ministry through providing various forms of day-
care.

Trust forms the foundations for all our relationships. Close relationships depend upon the ability to trust. Adults often test other
adults to determine their level of trustworthiness. If individuals prove
able to handle a small secret, then we will trust them with a larger
secret. If they prove their trustworthiness, we continue to be more
honest and open with them. Successful relationships, whether friend-
ship or marriage, demand the need for trust. A relationship with God
demands such trust. That does not mean that if we learn to view the
world as untrustworthy, we cannot trust God. However, the process
may be more difficult. If children can initially learn to trust the world
about them, we help prepare them for eventually trusting God.

Another crucial aspect of development is the interaction between
the child's development, parental style, and the relationship between
the parents. These three elements have a reciprocal influence upon
each other. For example, if the parents have had poor marital adjustments, this in turn is often reflected in their parenting style. The way
the parents interact with the child will affect the child's development.
If the child has developmental problems, then the parents may be affected in the quality of their marriage relationship and the subsequent
parenting skill behaviors. Thus, with the birth of the child, a network
of relationships is established that can affect marriage and family.[10]

In addition to emotional or social needs, the child is beginning to
experience rapid growth in locomotion and language skills. As the
child attempts to use these abilities, careful guidance and encouragement are needed. Locomotion and language skills prepare the child to
become an mature adult. Failure to encourage or to stimulate the
child may affect the overall reaching of developmental possibilities.

Learning Activity

1. Design a church program that will nurture and celebrate new births in your congregation. Be specific.
2. A group of concerned mothers has approached you concerning their young children (under two years of age). What can they do to prepare the way for their children becoming Christians at the appropriate time? What is your response?
3. Compare and contrast the bonding between mother and child and the bonding that occurs between God and humanity.

Preschool Years

These years are characterized by rapid growth in terms of cognitive and social abilities. The child is rapidly learning to stand and run. This increased locomotion brings about increased independence. Not without cause is the age of two often termed *the terrible twos.* The child is establishing his own identity, and one way of doing this is by saying no and doing things on one's own. While loudly exclaiming *no* and insisting upon doing things oneself may annoy parents, such practices are healthy because the child is trying to establish a sense of identity and consequent ability. One way of deciding who we are is to say who we are not.

Studies indicate that children that have secure attachments with parents, particularly the mother, tend to have better peer relations and better social skills than insecurely attached children. Poorly attached or insecurely attached children tend to be less secure in peer relationships and often find themselves as being either aggressive or passive in these relationships. Often children who are disruptive or who seem to always be the victim are suffering from an insecure attachment to a primary caregiver. These early relationships in life influence future life relationships.[11]

Play is an extremely important aspect of the child's life because it provides a natural medium for learning various skills such as communication, assuming leadership, cooperating, respecting the rights of others, and the use of imagination. The child undergoes various stages of play development that include unoccupied, solitary, onlooker, parallel, association, and finally cooperative play. Play provides an excellent medium through which the child can become acquainted with biblical truths such as fairness, justice, and concern for others. Play encourages both creativity and competency.

Another significant aspect of development is the learning of gender-typed behaviors. Various factors influence the development of these behaviors. Factors include biological factors—various hormonal and genetic factors; cognitive factors—beginning to classify one's sex and seeking to act out that label behaviorally; and environmental influences that include parents, teachers, and peers.[12] Through complex interaction, the child discovers what is appropriate and what is not.

In reference to the Christian faith, it is important to consider to what types of Christian models the child is exposed. In our society, Christian behaviors and virtues are often considered "feminine" or "weak." Quite possibly, the child may acquire the attitude that Christianity is restricted to the weak or to effeminate behavior. The church should provide living models with which children can identify.

As the child begins to approach the early school years, the five basic needs (relationship, knowledge, competency, creativity, and physiological satisfaction) begin to find expression. While all five needs are crucial, different ages and different individuals will meet the needs in various ways. How these needs are met will influence personality development. Deprivation or overindulgence of the needs to the neglect of other needs produces various personality types.

Early School Years

Piaget described various cognitive developmental stages through which the child grows. These stages reflect particular ways the child thinks, and give insight to Christian educators. While we may know clearly the content of what we teach, the receiving child may obtain content that is different from the original intent.

Piaget's preoperational child (two to seven) has a definite way of thinking, processing information, and viewing the world. One way the child thinks is animism—the giving of lifelike qualities to inanimate objects. For example, the child thinks his toys possess lifelike qualities. Another type of thinking involves the belief that wishing or make believe creates reality. The child also displays purposiveness—believing that whatever happens has a personal significance and purpose for him. The child is perception-bound in that he is only able to look at an object from the vantage of one quality or perspective. The child has not developed the various principles of conservation which involve the idea that mass is not altered by an alteration in appearance. The thought processes at this stage are highly egocentric.

The child understands things very literally. Care must be exercised during this time in the use of religious words and the conveying of religious truth. Religious symbols with which the adult is comfortable can cause great anxiety and confusion for the young child. In this time of developing schemata, prejudices may arise. For example, thinking of sin as black may set up a prejudice or prejudgment toward black people as sinful. In the instruction of the child, the use of highly symbolic language and imagery must be carefully avoided. Later, the child will be able to understand the symbolic quality.

One of the most endearing qualities of a child is high creativity and imagination. If properly nurtured, the child is excited about learning and exploring an ever-expanding world. The child has a youthful enthusiasm for the learning environment. The child's eyes can see what the adult's eyes may no longer witness—fresh appreciation and inquisitive joy. Tragically, the child's creativity may be damaged by nonbending structures or restrictions. Environments that do not encourage creativity may be found in the school, family, and church. Enforcing conformity on the learner may be easier to manage in light of limited resources and the need for unity. However, unlocking one's creativity involves loosing a part of one's God-given potentiality. The church should encourage the creative potential of each child.

Late School Years

During this stage (seven to eleven years), the child enters into what Piaget calls the Concrete Operational Period. Characteristics of this period include the ability to take the viewpoint of others. The child begins to realize there is more than one solution to a problem. He can understand that objects can belong to more than one classification at a time. In addition, the child acquires the various principles of conservation. The child is beginning to understand various mental operations. However, problem solving still needs reference to concrete objects. The child displays his increased abilities to deal with the world through more knowledge and mastery of skills.

According to Erikson, from age six to eleven the child is concerned with the developing of skills. Skill development has tremendous implications. Academic achievement and personality changes will be affected. Verbally gifted children tend to be more socially developed. Language allows us to communicate and to receive feedback; both aspects increase our possibility of positive social relationships.

Children, like their adult counterparts, need recognition and reinforcement for their sense of well-being. A great deal of our recognition goes to children who display high academic achievement and high athletic prowess. The child who does not achieve academic success or athletic prowess may be prone to drop out of school and to seek recognition or reinforcement in nonacceptable ways. The child may develop socially nonacceptable behavior in order to achieve a sense of relationships, competency, creativity, knowledge, and physiological satisfaction.

In despair, the nonacademically inclined child may relinquish his ability to achieve. Developing learned helplessness, the child may acquire an outlook that seeking to solve problems is useless; failure is inevitable. The local church may be the only place where the child may feel good about his achievements. While churches are not concerned with grades, the church should seek to aid its children to achieve their highest academic potential. Much of life is based upon the mastery of fundamental academic skills such as reading, writing, and arithmetic. Historically, the church has helped those with educational needs.

While much of a child's life is centered in the mastery of academic skills, there are other skills that are significant, and the church may help the child develop these skills. Children need to feel that their contributions are important and meaningful. Skills developed may not appear important or elaborate to an adult, nevertheless, they may have important implications.

The basic premise is that we are created for relationship (fellowship) with God; the end result of Christian education is the development of stewards. One of the greatest skills that we can help children develop is to know that they can do "something" for God. For the children, that "something" may involve carrying flags in the auditorium for Bible School. The children may learn that they can pray for missionaries or give money to buy Bibles, food, or clothing for other boys and girls. The church can teach that each individual can make a creative contribution to God. No gift, or life, is insignificant.

The child's world is changing from a family-centered to a nonfamily-centered approach. Increasing amounts of time are spent with other children and nonparental adults. Groups become very important. With a feeling of increased ability comes increased independence. Peer influence tends to become stronger and stronger. Strong peer identification at church may be instrumental in developing strong character and preparing the child for the changes of adolescence.

Characteristics of the self begin to change. As the child becomes aware of the viewpoints of others, he has an increased ability to understanding how he is viewed by others. At this point, he may have a deeper understanding of how he is viewed by his parents, Sunday School teacher, pastor, and even by God.

The child begins to have a more differentiated view of self. He realizes that he is not just good or bad. (This understanding is important to the adult, as well.) The individual can know that he may please God at times; other times, he may displease God. He is still the same person. Doing something bad one moment does not mean that the person cannot ever do good. Doing good does not mean that he will not do evil. Slowly, the child becomes personally aware of the complexities of the human condition.

According to Lawrence Kohlberg, the child has been operating on Level I of moral reasoning. This preconventional morality involves a reward-and-punishment orientation. The child does certain acts in order that to receive a reward and avoids other acts so as not to be punished. Later, Level II or conventional morality may be attained in which the child focuses upon something other than self, such as family, group, or nation.

This aspect of moral reasoning has implications for the Christian conversion process. Do we seek to have children respond to God on a reward/punishment orientation? Do we seek to have children respond to God on a love or gratitude orientation? Our practices or methodologies are extremely important because they tend to foster or encourage various types of orientations. Additionally, if service to God is encouraged and educationally fostered only out of a sense of reward or punishment, this pattern may continue through life.

Learning Activity 5.5

1. Children acquire their understanding of gender roles based upon their environment. Identify what you consider to be appropriate behavior for a female and appropriate behavior for a male. Are there behaviors that are appropriate for both sexes? If so, specify those behaviors.
2. Identify Christian roles that you believe are appropriate for the two sexes. Does your church actively support your beliefs? If not, what is your response?
3. Describe what you consider to be appropriate Christian truths for an early school-age child (five to seven years). How can these "truths" be appropriately taught to the child?
4. In the early school years, children display creativity. In later school years, children fail to display their former creativity. What

happens? Create a set of guidelines to encourage creativity among children through the school years.
5. Feeling successful is crucial to the development of a good self-concept. What can be done to ensure that each child feels a measure of success?
6. What activities can a child learn that he can do as a steward of God?
7. How would you explain the plan of salvation to a child of late school years?

Adolescence

Adolescence, the transition period from childhood to adulthood, is hard to define and to delineate in terms of specific ages. Adolescence may be described as beginning in biology (puberty) and ending in culture/society (when society acknowledges adult status with both privilege and responsibility). Adolescence is essentially a mark of a Western, technologically advanced society. With increased industrialization, the granting of adulthood status has been deferred more and more. In addition, the marks of adulthood vary from society to society and from specific adult activity to other activity.

In more primitive, agrarian societies, the mark from childhood to adulthood was more specific. Often there were marks of transition called rites of passage. Such was indeed the case with the Hebrews. For the male, the rite of passage was his thirteenth birthday and his bar mitzvah. Do rites of passage exist today within the Christian community?

The church needs to seek those activities that will celebrate the passage of adolescence to adulthood. This rite of passage may not be a specific event, but rather specific acts or activities marking the assumption of more and more responsibility. Just as society conveys its recognitions of adult status, the church should also recognize the new status achievements of its adolescents.

During this period of growth and development, the adolescent makes specific cognitive changes. Piaget termed this stage the Formal

Operational Period. Essentially, in this stage, the individual learns to "think like a scientist." This thinking involves the ability to observe facts; construct, test, and modify hypotheses, and, if needed, to retest. The increased need of knowledge applies to the spiritual dimension as well. The individual is able to ask adultlike questions regarding God, religious practice, and denominational structure. Answers need to match the intellectual level of the questions. The person who asks adult questions needs adult answers. Simple answers similar to those given to children are not appropriate. If given "unreasoned" answers, the individual may assume that the Sunday School answers or the church dogmas are pertinent only to children. Youth may not take seriously the challenges of the church and, most tragically, the challenges of Christ.

At this stage, youth develop the ability to reason about their own beliefs. Most importantly, they may begin to realize what is truly biblical and what is denominational or cultural bias. For this important step in growth of faith, solid Bible study is essential. Only in discovering the essence of Christianity can real Christianity become a solid part of one's maturing faith. If this reasoning does not occur, the person may mix biblical faith and cultural bias to the extent that he or she is not able to distinguish between the two. In the process, the essence of the gospel that frees humankind may be lost. The shadow may be followed, but the essence may be lost. Youth must be challenged to think and to think biblically.

Often youth may experience doubt about their church and their own professions of faith. The church must continue to devote its loving concern to those who doubt their faith. Rather than viewing this religious doubt or questioning as harmful, the church can view doubting as an opportunity for the growth of a more genuine and mature faith. Few important lessons in life are learned without struggle or discomfort. Educationally, the schemata are in tension. The adolescent needs guidance in reconciling the schemata. Honest answers and a genuine relationship are crucial in formulating a mature faith.

Youth develop a type of egocentrism in which they believe that everyone is as concerned with them as they are with themselves. Every blemish becomes a major trauma. They believe that everyone else is just as preoccupied with the blemish as they are. Adolescents believe that they are playing or dramatizing their lives to an audience. They are on the center of the stage. Being on center stage causes a great deal of anxiety; such anxiety needs reassurance. Youth need teachers and adult leadership who understand the importance of the changing qualities of the adolescent.

An adolescent thinks idealistically. Typically, he believes that no one has ever felt as intensely as he does. In addition, he is very much looking for something to which to commit his life, something or someone that can give a sense of meaning or purpose. The adolescent may find that the church is the place where such meaning is found.

Tragically, if youth do not find the church as a place of meaning, they will search elsewhere, perhaps in less desirable places. Cults may provide the type of fellowship that is so very important for the adolescent. The church should prepare for admitting its youth into more adultlike places of meaning and responsibility so adolescents may offer their lives in service to God.

In addition, the adolescent period, according to Erikson, involves the search for identity. Early in this period the identity is chiefly concerned with sexual identity. Marked differences in biology are occurring as a result of puberty and the maturation process. Much of adolescent attention is directed toward satisfying the sensate or physiological needs. Guidance is needed at this time in order that the physiological needs may be handled in a healthy, Christian fashion. Continued sexual education is needed from a Christian perspective.

Psychological implications emerge as a result of these physiological changes. Early and late maturers are often affected by the changes. The early maturing female may have difficulty in relating to her class and peer group. Additionally, the early maturing female may be attracted to older males who are beyond her in emotional stability. The early maturing male may be in a somewhat more advantageous position. He may be more apt to be selected as the leader in school elections, as well as on the athletic field.

The late maturing male may have the most difficult position in the process. Not only is the late maturing male behind all of his male peers but also his female peers in size. In addition, teachers have a tendency to treat one as an adult if one has the physical stature of an adult. This idea has implications for both the male and the female. While a female may be fully developed physically, she may still be a young girl in her emotions and her cognitions. A male, if he is underdeveloped physically, may be emotionally and cognitively more fully developed. Abilities must not be underestimated or overestimated.

The church should provide opportunities for fellowship among the sexes. As a rule, youth will find fellowship with the opposite sex. The questions may be: Where will they find that fellowship, and under what value systems or support system? To deny this important part of life may alienate the youth from the church or may cause them to experience a part of the world that may make return to the church more difficult. Patience and care are necessary.

The latter part of the struggle, according to Erikson, concerns itself with vocational identity. The church can do a great deal to aid adolescents making vocational choices. Rather than stressing full-time Christian service, the church would do well to emphasize the universal call to a life of Christian service, regardless of the particular job or profession.

The church should aid the youth in their quest for vocational identity. One way of doing this is exploring options. This idea needs to be clearly expressed and expanded. It is crucial for the church to allow its youth to explore the world of work, and then to decide how they might best live out their Christian lives. For some, this may involve full-time service in a specific church vocation. For others, this call might involve secular work. Both sacred and secular work are valuable if one follows God's leadership.

A word of caution is needed. Youth are particularly sensitive to church leaders, whether it be pastor, music leader, or youth director. Consequently, youth may be persuaded to follow a church vocation because of the character or charm of the leader. While this is acceptable in initially exploring a church-related position, it is crucial that individuals be God-called and not leader-called or self-called. Tremendous emphasis should be placed upon the idea that abundant Christian life can be found among many vocational choices. Youth may be called into full-time business, just as they might be called to full-time Christian service.

Youth have the potential for giving great strength, integrity, and ideology to the church. A question appropriately raised is: Will the church provide those open opportunities, guidance, and integrity that youth need and demand? The youth carry the future of the church. The adolescent period is preoccupied with the five basic needs: physiological satisfaction, fellowship, knowledge, competency, and creativity. How the church assists youth in meeting those needs will influence the life of the youth, as well as the life of the church.

Learning Activity 5.6

1. List "rites of passage" that marked your transition to more adult-like responsibility.
2. What does your church currently do to mark the passage of adolescence to adulthood? What suggestions would you have for commemorating this passage into adulthood?
3. You have been working with your youth group for several years. Some of the youth are beginning to express "questions" about the Christian faith. Several parents are expressing their concern to you. What is your response?
4. Sexual identity and vocational identity are central issues for adolescence. Design a program that will allow these needs to be ministered to in a Christian context.
5. As the youth minister, several adolescents have expressed interest in becoming ministers of youth. How do you respond to their interest, as well to the interest of other adolescents seeking a vocational identity?
6. Plan a summer of experiences for high-school juniors and seniors

that will help them in their vocational search.

Young Adulthood

According to Erikson, young adulthood involves the search for intimacy versus isolation. Generally, young adulthood is a time for searching for intimacy with the opposite sex. Genuine intimacy can only be achieved if one has achieved a sense of identity. Marriages are failing. People are failing in their attempts to achieve intimacy. Physical intimacy is relatively easy to achieve. However, emotional intimacy is another matter. Identity must precede intimacy.

The church may help in achieving this emotional intimacy by allowing individuals to experience intimacy with themselves through unconditional acceptance by God. Real identity can be found only in stewardship to the Creator. Only when we feel accepted are we willing to take off personality masks and camouflages. Only when we can admit our hurts, our deepest feelings, and our strengths, as well as weaknesses, can we learn to be intimate with another human. The process of intimacy may begin in a step-by-step unveiling.

This need for intimacy must not be restricted to sexual union or marriage. Rather, intimacy involves the opening or the allowing of another person to participate in our innermost selves. Single adults, whether always single or single again, need opportunities for intimacy. The church can provide an environment in which genuine fellowship may be experienced.

While married adults confront loneliness, the single is at a particular disadvantage in the church. Church is a family-oriented institution. Does one individual constitute a family? Church programming activities tend to be family or couple oriented. What about the single? Is the single the abnormal? Are singles in their twenties, thirties, and forties treated as full adults? Are such individuals allowed to assume appropriate levels of adult leadership? Providing opportunities for genuine relationship with God, self, and others applies to all.

Theorists say there may be a fifth stage of cognitive development beyond Piaget's formal operational period. One theorist, Gisela Labouvie-Vief, suggests that the thinking of the young adult is more pragmatic and contextual in nature. Often replacing the adolescent's surge of idealism and abstract thinking, adult thinking takes on a much more immediate and pragmatic focus. Adults are concerned with finding their own positions in a complex world.[13] Adults seek to prove their own competency and knowledge in various chosen areas. Some adults may center their thinking around their professional or vocational commitments. Concerns may change from feeding the world or developing a world vision to balancing one's monthly income or planning a meal for in-laws.

Young adults may be concerned with developing their full potential. Often "full potential" is defined in terms of maximum financial earnings. Climbing to the top may assume a tremendous role in the life of young adults. In fact, individuals may neglect their relationships with spouses, children, and church in the pursuit of the "good life." While this is a tremendously healthy period of life for them, they may begin to develop bad health habits. Essentially, they may "burn" the candle at both ends. In the process, life may later suffer because of this undisciplined or unnurturing life-style.

An important part of the Christian faith is the idea that all of life involves the growing recognition of God's ownership. Such ownership is not restricted to the past or future. Rather, ownership involves the present. Too often the young adult is apt to postpone valuable areas of life that should not be taken for granted. The working father may neglect his relationship with wife and children for "success at work" only to find there is no family left intact. The individual may postpone demonstrating his financial stewardship to God. Later he may discover that he has financially overcommitted himself to such an extent that financial obedience to God is more difficult.

The young adult is generally concerned with establishing and maintaining a family. Not all have been fortunate in having good family models on which to base their own family style. More mature families can provide the living model for newly created families. Church support and instruction can help parents establish those values that were important or missing in their own lives.

A tendency exists for families to generate knowledge and behavior from one generation to the next. Family relations and behaviors tend to be repeated from one generation to the next. Child abuse experienced by one generation often reappears in the next generation. It is not difficult to understand why this happens. We tend to act in light of past adult models. The male who watches his mother physically abused by his father may grow up to be a male who treats his own wife in a similar fashion. The relationship between a mother and her child often reflects the relationship between herself and her mother. The cycle continues.

However, a vicious cycle of negative behaviors can be altered. Conscious intervention is needed. Humans have a tendency to repeat history on both a national as well as an individual level. The church can provide a magnificent witness in testifying to Christ's resurrection, to the changed life brought about by one's commitment to Him, and commitment to maturing in Christlike fashions. Those who have broken the cycle of poor family relations may offer hope and direction to others.

In ministering to young adults, the focal concerns of their lives must be utilized. These adults tend to be problem oriented with limited amounts of available time and energy. Christian educational programming must meet genuine needs. Something of value must be offered. These adults have achieved a degree of knowledge and competency; the church must utilize this giftedness in creative expressions of ministry. The church must seek to help the young adults discover their present-day stewardship and relationship to God.

Activity 5.7

1. List focal concerns of the young adult.
2. What are special needs of the married young adult and the single young adult?
3. What is the appropriate role for the young adult in church life?
4. Young adults are failing to become more than marginally involved

in church life. Hypothesize reasons and solutions for this situation.

Middle Adulthood

Marked physical changes occur in middle adulthood. Various sensory changes occur; compensation is often made for the declines. Generally there is a gradual decline in the ability of the eyes to accommodate; typically eyeglasses are required. Hearing, especially sensitivity to high-pitched sounds, may be affected. Speaking in a lower-pitched voice may help the individual; hearing aids may also be appropriately used. Generally, a decline occurs in physical strength, endurance, and reaction time. The individual may need to adjust to lessened physical abilities and reaction times. Sexual changes also occur.

With such physical and subsequent emotional changes, middle adults become especially sensitive to their physical health. Persons often assume renewed responsibility for their lives in such areas as weight control and exercise. In fact, the middle-age adult may begin a regimented physical-education program in the hope of fighting off the aging process. With the deaths of friends, parents, and other family members, these persons become increasingly aware of their own mortality and health concerns such as heart disease and cancer.

Sexual changes produce significant adjustments for both sexes. Typically, the female experiences menopause, the cessation of menstruation, around the age of fifty. The time of onset is often related to heredity. This event itself can be particularly painful for a female whose value has been centered around her sexuality in terms of physical attractiveness or the ability to bear children. The female may be especially vulnerable to negative evaluations of her personhood.

New avenues to display competency, creativity, and knowledge are needed. Christian faith and nurturance can add much to her adjustment to this new phase of life. Reemphasizing that "there is neither male nor female; for you are all one in Christ Jesus" (Gal. 3:28) may help in the realization that worth, value, or identity expands far beyond physical sexuality. The essence of personhood is more than sexual. Loving concern is needed by this woman from her husband, family, and church.

For the male, waning physical powers, including sexual activity, may be a source of constant concern. The male may attempt to regain his youth through new clothes, new modes of transportation, new hobbies, divorce, extramarital relations, or new vocational choices. He may need to find and to redefine his own identity in Christ. Both the male and the female need support. While the church should not be alarmed by harmless attempts to recapture youth, such as a new car, new clothes, or new hobbies, the church also has a preventive ministry in educating the individual to find new value and strength in life. Life should look forward and not backward.

The middle-aged parent is faced with a unique challenge of becoming a parent to her own parents. This new parenting produces a new added dimension to her life. Parenting one's parents is especially exhausting should the parents face illness and disability requiring constant care. In addition, her own children are leaving home and are in the process of becoming parents themselves. The church can seek to provide definite ministries to the middle-aged individual. Church visiting/ministry teams may be mobilized to visit and care for the aging parents in order to allow relief for adults who must administer such constant care.

Erikson's term for this stage of development is generativity versus stagnation. Generativity refers to an individual's interest in or concern for the next generation. Either the individual will invest a part of his life in the loving care of the next generation, or he will stagnate and become self-centered. To become interested in the next generation offers many new opportunities for creative service and fulfillment. In a Christian context, exercising care for the next generation is a part of discipleship. Christians have opportunity to guide the lives of younger Christians. In the process of guiding other lives, middle-age adults are guiding their own lives toward fulfillment and positive evaluation. Guiding others by showing knowledge, competency, and fellowship can be one of the most creative expressions of life possible.

Robert Peck expanded Erikson's generativity stage to include the conflict between wisdom and physical power, socializing versus sexualizing in human relationships, cathectic flexibility versus cathectic impoverishment, and mental flexibility versus mental rigidity. According to Peck, the question arises if the individual is able to move from the latter issue to the former issue or tendency. Rather than focusing upon diminishing physical powers, the adult can focus on the growth of wisdom that can nurture future life. The possibility exists for viewing humans in terms of socializing relationships rather than sexualizing, which may be characteristic of an earlier age. Cathectic bonds may be strengthened as the individual looks forward to new relationships, not focusing upon the past. Individuals may choose to keep their mental outlook and activities open to new experiences, rather than fixed upon past understandings and experiences.[14]

While middle age may be viewed as a last opportunity to postpone the aging process, this position is not consistent with a biblical understanding of life. Life is a progression that seeks to mature in understanding and application. Rather than attempting to keep life at a standstill, a person must look forward toward valued maturity. Looking forward to life involves an open mind-set and life-style. Scripture records that people who lose their vision perish. This truth applies not only on a national level but also on an individual level. While the physical vision and activity of the middle-aged adult may diminish, spiritual vision and activity may actually increase. New expressions for relationships, including knowledge, competency, and creativity, exist. These needs find fulfillment in forward activity.

Learning Activity 5.8

1. Compare and contrast the world's view of aging to a biblical view.
2. Search the Scriptures for middle and older adults who made significant contributions to God's work.
3. Search the Scriptures for biblical truths that can aid adults as they enter the middle-adult years.
4. Interview a middle-age adult in your church. Focus on his or her dreams for the church, as well as any words to the younger

generation.

Aging Adult

Aging is a complex phenomenon. Various theories exist to explain aging. Aging may be examined from a biological perspective. Body cells may be limited with respect to the number of times they may divide. Increasing age may affect the body's immune system so that the body no longer is able to regulate its own growth. On one level, aging may be explained by such various physiological mechanisms.

While there are presently definite limits to what can be done biologically for the aging process, sociological perspectives may provide more stimulation and direction for those interested in the Christian faith and education. Three basic sociological theories of aging include: disengagement theory, activity theory, and social breakdown-reconstruction theory. Each of these theories will be described and followed by analysis for Christian educational considerations.

Disengagement theory espouses that as persons become older, they naturally and gradually withdraw from society. In turn, society begins to "disengage" itself from the individual. This view is considered the normal process of aging. As the person becomes disengaged, there is a resulting increased self-preoccupation, weakening of emotional ties with others, and diminishing interest in the affairs of others.

Activity theory states that the more active and involved, the greater life satisfaction and the less likely to age. Persons are more likely to remain youthful sociologically if they are actively involved in life. To fight aging one must be active, not passive. Although certain roles and opportunities may be lost with increasing age, it is crucial that the individuals find appropriate substitute roles to fulfill their new lives.

Social breakdown-reconstruction theory states that aging is the result of various sociological and psychological forces that influence each other. Aging is promoted through negative psychological functioning that involves poor self-concept, negative feedback from others and society, and a lack of skills to deal with the world. The social system itself contributes to the aging process. This social system can be altered by promoting a positive value, regard, or appreciation for the aging.[15]

The sociological theories illustrate that aging is much more than a decline in physiological functioning. While limited physically in dealing with the aging process, we can socially or psychologically deal with the process. With its rich structure and systems, the church can have a significant impact upon its view of the senior adult. The contributions of senior adults should be fully utilized. They offer a tremendous potential for the church in terms of experience and commitment. At the same time, senior adults have a tremendous need to show their competencies and creative service.

Disengagement theory stresses that it is normal for an individual to become less interested in the affairs of others with increasing age. However, Christian faith is relationship oriented. Therefore, no part of the Christian life span is unconcerned with relationships. In fact, senior adults may be limited physically with what they can do in terms of physical strength and travel. However, through prayer and study, senior adults may find the world opening once again as children do when they read books and travel with their imagination. In fact, they can use their prayers to lift themselves to lives and lands beyond their immediate awareness. Rather than becoming less interested in the affairs of the world, senior adults may have the time to pray and to participate in mission projects that shape and mold the face of the world.

The church should be willing to mobilize the forces of its senior citizens for great works of God. John Wesley, for example, was an aging man who spent a great deal of time on horseback, traveling and preaching the gospel. The elderly may not be able to preach and travel to faraway places; however, they can be involved in world events and in gospel proclamation wherever they are. Many mission activities and projects can allow the elderly to share one of the most important ingredients in Christian witnessing, the art of time spent in fellowship.

Individuals often have positive regard for their grandparents; grandparents show their love through interest and time spent. The

aging Christian has an opportunity to "grandparent" other generations. The aging apostle John wrote to his congregation: "Love one
another, just as he has commanded us" (1 John 3:23). In this process,
the love may become more and more real.

Aging individuals often engage in a life review in which they look
back over their lives. This life review need not be regarded as negative;
it has various positive elements. It allows individuals to consolidate
their own viewpoints of their lives; it allows for the possible resolution
of past unresolved conflicts; it allows for a realistic appraisal of one's
worth and present vulnerability, and it may allow for a realization of
past actions and the desire to make new commitments.[16]

Life review may require the listening ear of the church family. In
addition, the church may need to give encouragement to those engaged in a life review. If new actions or commitments are required,
then encouragement and support may be needed in order for that to
become a reality. The aging need reminding of the new life that awaits
those who have trusted in Christ as Lord and Savior. Focusing on the
promises of God can lead them to face the beginning of a new phase of
life and existence.

Retirement is another issue that the aging person must accept.
Those who are most successful in retirement are those who are able to
substitute roles and activities for previous ones. The church can provide new activities for the well-being of its aging congregation. Programs of travel, study, and mission activity may give new reason and
hope for the aging.

The church should be willing to become involved with the growing
needs of the aging in terms of their physical existence. Such concerns
include housing, transportation, nutrition, and health. As the church
ministers to the needs of its aging adults, it is giving a positive witness
for all generations, especially the new generation that will care or not
care for them. By our own role modeling, we are constantly creating
the church of the future.

While the church contributes to the care of the aging, the church
must not overlook the positive contributions that aging persons can

make to the church. The witness at the first steps of faith are as significant as the witness of the later steps of faith. All steps of faith are worthy of example and inspiration.

Learning Activity 5.9

1. Compare the disengagement theory, the social-breakdown theory, and the activity theory. Which one(s) appear(s) more biblically sound? Explain.
2. What is the current role of older adults in your church?
3. What are some ministry opportunities to aging adults in your community?

Death

Can there be teaching or Christian education when someone dies? Without question, the church teaches a message about life as it deals with deaths of its members. Through various rituals—the funeral service, memorial gifts, and preparing a meal for the family—the church is teaching about life. If the church offers gifts of appropriate appreciation for the Christian life of its members, it teaches that one's influence continues.

Various needs that motivate and direct our behavior have been explored. These include the need for physiological satisfaction, relationships, knowledge, creativity, and competency. Each of these basic needs can be perverted. Proper balance can be found only in the lordship of Christ. These needs manifest themselves throughout the life span. Death may reveal how an individual has demonstrated the meeting of these needs.

Just as the church celebrates in the birth of the young, the church should celebrate in the death of her members. The death of a life lived under Christ's lordship should provide encouragement and direction for those still in the process of living. Life may be regarded as a preparation for the life to come; death is the transition to the new life and identity. Through belief in Christ, death has lost its sting.

Teaching and learning occur throughout the entire life cycle. The

Christian faith is committed to the spread of the gospel and to the nurturing of those with whom it comes into contact. Therefore, no aspect of life is impervious to the gospel. To be engaged in Christian education is to be engaged in teaching through the generations, as well as throughout the generation.

Learning Activity 5.10

1. What should be the Christian response to the death of its members? Be specific.
2. Have you ever experienced the death of a Christian to whom you were especially close? Describe that response. What did you learn in the experience?
3. Discuss how the Christian faith can be encouraged across the life-span.

Notes

1. John W. Santrock, *Life Span Development*, 3d ed. (Dubuque, Iowa: Wm. C. Brown Co., Publishers, 1989), 275-76.

2. See Lawrence Kohlberg, *Essays on Moral Development, Volume I: The Philosophy of Moral Development: Moral Stages and the Idea of Justice*, and *Volume II: The Psychology of Moral Development: The Nature and Validity of Moral Stages* (San Francisco: Harper & Row, Publishers, 1981).

3. For further study see Donald M. Joy, ed., *Moral Development Foundations: Judeo-Christian Alternatives to Piaget/Kohlberg* (Nashville: Abingdon Press, 1983).

4. See Erik H. Erikson, *The Life Cycle Completed: A Review* (New York: W. W. Norton & Company, 1982).

5. Wayne E. Oates, *The Psychology of Religion* (Waco: Tex.: Word Books, 1973), 67-71.

6. James S. Fowler, *Stages of Faith: The Psychology of Human Development and the Quest for Meaning* (New York: Harper & Row, 1981).

7. Otto Friedrich, "What Do Babies Know?" *Time*, 15 August 1983, 52-59.

8. A. Christine Harris, *Child Development* (St. Paul: West Publishing Company, 1986), 82-84.

9. Santrock, 189-93.

10. Ibid., 188-89.

11. Ibid., 191-92.

12. Ibid., 270-75.

13. Gisela Labouvie-Vief, "Dynamic Development and Mature Autonomy," *Human Development* 25 (May-June 1982): 161-91.

14. Peck as cited in John W. Santrock, *Life-Span Development*, 2d ed. (Dubuque: Iowa: Wm. C. Brown Co., Publishers, 1983), 496.
15. Santrock, 537-38.
16. Margaret H. Huyck and William J. Hoyer, *Adult Development and Aging* (Belmont, Calif.: Wadsworth Publishing Company, 1982), 152-53.

6
Three Reflections of Christian Education: Family, Church, and School

An Overview of the Relationship Theme

Various social groups and institutions exist today that demonstrate goals and behaviors similar to the church, school, and the Christian family. The distinctiveness of these three institutions resides in their special relationship to God and how they seek to promote that relationship in others. Involved in the distinctive qualities are their primary acknowledgment of God, a place of hearing God's Word, teaching that we are not alone, teaching obedient love to God, instilling a new identity in Christ, teaching the importance of modeling God's love, providing opportunities for mature growth and service, involving all members in continual instruction, choosing appropriate behaviors to convey its message, and utilizing the power of the Holy Spirit. The strength and power of the Christian family, the church, and the school reside in their relationship to God.

Introduction

One of the basic questions asked in Christian education is in what context should the process of education occur. Christian education can flourish in many places. Several years ago, a Christian college class was conducted in the confines of a prison. Was this the proper atmosphere for Christian education? Upon analysis, the answer is yes.

Christian education is not restricted to any one particular building or ecclesiastical structure. In fact, the world itself is the classroom for Christian education. Three traditional structures give expression to

Christian education: the family, the church, and the school. Each has its common characteristics, and each has its special differences. Following discussion of the unique characteristics of these institutions, general discussion will be given concerning some biblical imperatives for the process of Christian education.

Family

The oldest societal institution is the family. Once, the extended family was the norm, where all members lived in close proximity and contributed to its maintenance. With increased mobility and technological advances, the extended family is no longer the norm. The nuclear family is the norm. Even within the nuclear family, the structure is changing. With increased divorce, single-parent homes are becoming more commonplace.

Development of the Modern Family.—As the oldest social institution, the family has been shaped by various social forces. Families provide the context by which societies regulate sexual behavior and provide for the socialization of children. However, forms of family life vary from society to society and culture to culture. While some cultures demand monogamy, others permit polygamy. On occasion, the family is patriarchal; other families are matriarchal.

In light of Western society, attention must be drawn to the Roman Catholic Church. From the fifth century A.D., the most influential institution in European life was the Roman Catholic Church. The Catholic Church influenced every facet of life, including marriage and family. The church was strict in its interpretation of human sexual behavior. Sex was regarded as sinful; premarital and extramarital sex were forbidden. Even in the context of marriage, the primary purpose of sex was strictly for procreation. Marrying for love was not common. Marriages were often prearranged for nonromantic reasons, including physical security, safeguarding family fortunes, procurement of heirs, and perpetuating family names.[1]

Romantic love, which our present society emphasizes intensely, did not gain any measure of popularity until the beginning of the High

Middle Ages. Until this time, women were regarded as little more than property. A female began first as the property of her father and then became the property of her husband. In the twelfth century, courtly love developed at the court of Eleanor of Aquitaine (1122-1204). This courtly love emphasized the importance of romance, honor, devotion, and adventure.

John Drakeford lists three major implications of the development of the idea of courtly love: (1) Courtly love enhanced the image of womanhood. No longer to be viewed as property, women were to be courted. The woman was to become the guiding light in the heart of her suitor and husband. (2) Courtly love refined ideas regarding sexual expression. While the emphasis in courtly love was the ideal, new focus was given to the importance of personal attraction in love and marriage. (3) Courtly love emphasized new character and ethical values. Involved in this emphasis was a new stress on good manners, devotion, and self-denial. This new emphasis was introduced in a world known for being cruel and crude. Courtly love began to transform mankind from a level of pure physical desire to a higher ethical standard of conduct.[2]

During the Protestant Reformation, newly established churches adopted less-restrictive views of marriage and family life than those of the Roman Catholic Church. One highly influential group in America, the English-speaking Puritans, emphasized that sex within marriage was good because it strengthened the marriage relationship. Individuals were encouraged to select their own mates. In the late seventeenth and eighteenth centuries, romantic attraction became an important factor in mate selection in both England and the United States. By the early-nineteenth century, marriage for love was a part of the norm.

Technological advances began to have impact upon the life of the family. Advances in medicine lowered infant mortality and increased the life span. At the beginning of the Industrial Revolution, the average number of children born to a woman was seven or eight. The Industrial Revolution significantly impacted social relationships, particularly marriage and the role of women. Women were no longer needed solely in the home for the production of goods such as cloth and processing food. Women transferred into factories where their services were needed in running the ever-expanding machinery. Parental control was lessened as women interacted freely with male co-workers. Individuals became more involved in mate selection than did their parents.

The Victorian age of the nineteenth century fostered a very conservative understanding of sex. The Victorians sought to hide human interest in sex. In the twentieth century, more relaxed views of sex and marriage arose. Following World War I, industrialization increased in the United States. Many people flocked to the cities where religious influence was less pronounced. Restrictions on social behavior, including marriage, were lessened.[3]

After the stock market crash of 1929, the United States entered the Great Depression. In this time of great economic stress, some of the loosened social behaviors were momentarily curtailed. Youth of the 1930s entered marriage later in life and had fewer children than their parents and grandparents. These youth of this period made the transition from childhood to adulthood without knowing the carefree days of adolescence. In later life, these depression children were characterized as cautious, conservative, and preoccupied with financial security.

Post-World-War-II America was particularly prosperous and powerful. While women typically worked outside the home during the war, these women returned to work in the home following the war years. The baby boom occurred during the decade following World War II. In this time of prosperity, the sharp rise in births resulted in more housing, churches, and schools.[4]

Today the family is characterized by increased geographic mobility, high divorce rates, and weakened family ties. Open marriage and cohabitation have become more commonplace. Both parents typically work. Children often spend long periods of time in day-care centers. The fabric of today's family is being held together by frail threads.

Christian Distinctives of the Family.—The Bible presents a clear view of the importance of the family, especially as it relates to national identity and to an identity with God Himself. The family tie was made sacred from the first by God's act in giving man and woman to each other (Gen. 1—3). In the act of creation, God created man and determined that it was not good that man should be alone. God created other living creatures. However, each of these creatures was not the appropriate companion for man. Therefore, God created woman.

Genesis 2:24 states: "Therefore a man leaves his father and his mother and cleaves to his wife, and they become one flesh." This verse indicates the importance of the new relationship's priority. When two individuals marry, they come from two distinct families. In the process of marriage, they are to create a new identity: a new family. In order for a successful new entity to emerge, it is important that new priorities be set. For this reason, a man must leave his family and cleave or bond to his wife. In this process of forming new relationships and loyalties, a new family is formed. Through the process of new families being formed, there is a sense in which the earth is replenished.

In studying Scripture, three apparent purposes for marriage and family arise. As previously discussed, one of the primary purposes is for companionship (Gen. 2:18-20). A second is the expression of love and sexual fulfillment (1 Cor. 7:3-5). The third purpose is for the provision of children (Gen. 1:27-28).

While Scripture addresses three basic purposes in marriage, Christian marriage may be summarized by the words "relational responsibilities." The relationship of husband and wife involves forsaking all other relationships (Eph. 5:31; Gen. 2:24), providing sexual satisfaction (1 Cor. 7:3-5), and remaining faithful to the marriage commitment (1 Cor. 7:10-11). In regard to children, the parents are to love (Titus 2:4), to educate (Deut. 6:6-7), to discipline (Eph. 6:4; Prov. 13:24; 19:18), to be kind (Col. 3:21), and to provide for basic needs (1 Tim. 5:8). The responsibility for relationship is not solely that of the parents; the children are also responsible. In Ephesians 6:1-3, children are instructed to honor and obey their parents. Additionally, children are to care for their parents (Mark 7:10-13), even as Jesus commanded the care of His mother.

As revealed in this survey, a high degree of mutual responsibility in relationship is emphasized in Scripture. Specific guidelines for living the relationship are offered. One of the greatest distinctives found in the Christian family, as well as in the church and Christian colleges, is the quality of relationship. The context of the relationship is established by God. Just as Christ called the church into being, God called the family into being. There is a sense in which the Christian family is a reflection of the church; and the church itself a reflection of the family. Both require Christ in order to live up to the distinctive claims. No Christ, no Christian family. No Christ, no church.

One of the families of the earth that has consistently maintained its identity has been that of the Hebrews or the Jewish people. Their family life has been central in their survival in spite of years of oppression and persecution. In all their persecution, the Jewish people never failed to remember their distinctiveness as the called of God. As Christians, we share in the heritage of the Hebrews and the messages that God spoke to them. We may not be the "original" chosen people in one sense of the word, but in another sense, because of our relationship with Christ, we are the new people through whom God has chosen to bless the world. Just as some Jews lost their distinctiveness when they courted other gods, we may lose our distinctiveness when we fail to live in loving family relationships to the one true God.

Learning Activity 6.1

1. List phrases that adequately describe the family in the twentieth century.
2. What are biblical truths regarding the Christian family?
3. What are some values that were taught to you in the context of your family?
4. What specific values would you want to teach your own family?

Colleges

The first two chapters of this work have discussed the significance of the Christian school and its historical development. A few additional comments will be made regarding its distinctive nature.

With respect to Christian schools, it is essential that schools maintain the philosophical and theological intent behind their founding. A Christian school should not be like any other school. In colonial America, early colleges and universities were established in order to provide trained clergyman and other leaders for the ever-growing American colonies. Many of these flourished and survive today. An appropriate question to ask is if these colleges and universities fulfill their originally assigned task. While flourishing in terms of academic reputation and prestige, some of the colleges have failed to maintain their distinctive Christian qualities. While it may be argued that to promote learning in an open environment is Christian, the question remains: Is there more to a Christian college than promoting an excellence in learning?

Ben C. Fisher argues that Christian colleges suffer great damage when basic biblical and theological presuppositions are neglected. He declares that the basis for Christian education involves the nature of God, truth, and human nature and destiny. (Fisher asks relationship questions.) Because God is the Source of all truth, as we study we discover more and more of God's creation. Higher education seeks to help human beings acquire tools to discover the truth of God and its subsequent implications for life.

In addition to its theological and biblical presuppositions, Fisher adds additional distinctives about Christian higher education. Christian colleges have an opportunity to convey true values from an unchanging God, to witness of the gospel, to train all in the discipleship of sharing the gospel, to integrate faith and learning, and to serve as a leavening or balancing force in society with a dual tract of higher education.[5]

The Christian college differs most distinctly from other institutions of higher learning in the quality of its relationships. Based upon its understanding of God's relationship to humanity and humanity's need for God, the Christian college is built upon a relationship that endures. Life and practice follow. To rid itself of its relationship to God is to deprive itself of its life-giving distinctiveness. As he passed the reins of responsibility, B. H. Carroll, president of Southwestern Baptist Theological Seminary, requested L. R. Scarborough, his successor, to "keep the seminary lashed to the cross."[6] In understanding the cross, we come to understand life and its intended directions. Such advice would be well taken by institutions which are identified as Christian.

Unless the Christian school has exceptional endowments, it is not possible for the small Christian school to compete with other schools in terms of funding and programming. However, the Christian school offers an important distinctive. The school provides an environment in which a Christian world view may be developed. Such a Christian perspective will guide the individual in studying, choosing a vocational alternative, and finding one's life in service to God and others. To help students find and to equip their lives in light of God's plan is the greatest contribution the Christian college can make.

One basic principle involved in learning is discovering one's gifts and seeking to develop that giftedness. Simply stated, be who you are; do not waste your resources on being who you are not. The Christian college has distinctive qualities that no other institution can offer. There is no need to be apologetic. If the Christian school tries to compete with public colleges and universities in terms of social freedom and lax moral restraints, the distinctiveness is lost. Jesus said: "For what will it profit a man, if he gains the whole world and forfeits his life" (Matt. 16:26)? The world of learning can be acquired, but life is lost without Christian commitment. Christian colleges can promote commitment that leads to eternal life.

Learning Activity 6.2

1. What should be the differences between a Christian school and a non-Christian school? What should be the similarities?
2. On one side of a sheet of paper, list the positive arguments for sending a child to a Christian school. On the other side, list the negative arguments for sending a child to a Christian school. Draw your own conclusions.
3. Should funding and focus be upon higher levels of Christian education (college/university level) or on the lower levels (kindergarten, elementary schools)? Explain.

Church

The church was called into existence, and is a product of the work of the Holy Spirit. The word *church* comes from the Greek word *ek klesia* composed of two words *ek* (out) and *kalein* (to call). *Ekklesia* refers to "the called out ones" or "assembly." The New Testament references to the church are either to a local group of baptized believers or the redeemed believers of all ages.[7]

The foundation of the church is Christ Himself (1 Cor. 3:11). Involved within the church are persons who, through their belief in Christ, have entered into the relationship of the church. The church involves individuals who are in fellowship with Christ and other believers. Because of this relationship with Christ, the relationship toward others outside of the church is characterized by love. The church fosters and encourages a new relationship—a new identity. Believers are indeed unique, different from the rest of the world.

To a large degree the church has accepted the model proposed by secular education for its educational programming. For example, Sunday School groupings generally reflect the age groupings employed in secular education. While such a decision may be correct, the church must not arbitrarily make its educational decisions based upon those made in secular education.

One of the key goals in Christian education should be promoting

Christian growth. Promoting such growth involves creativity and flexibility. This does not mean lack of order, nor does it mean automatic chaos. Of all agencies, the church should be free to develop educational programming that will benefit the church body. Too often a program perpetuates itself and loses its basic purposes. For example, we may become so involved in "doing" Sunday School that we forget the reason for the existence of Sunday School.

Different historical contexts have demanded different educational programming to meet genuine human need. While creativity and flexibility are necessary, guidelines are also necessary. The guidelines that should direct the church's educational ministry are the theological and philosophical foundations and the mission of the church. In seminary education, one basic question deals with the basic nature of the church: What is the church? Once one has explored that question from various vantage points, the guidelines or philosophies of operation emerge.

Each church or denomination itself must answer this vital question. For example, Southern Baptists identify four functions of the church based upon its mission: worship; proclaim and witness; nurture and educate; and minister.[8] To worship involves a personal encounter with God in which the Christian experiences a deepening of faith and strengthening of service. To proclaim and witness involves the proclaiming of God's redemption in Christ so that all might believe. To nurture and educate involves guiding individuals in their progressive development toward Christian maturity. To minister involves the meeting of humans needs in the spirit of Christ.

Once the areas of the biblical foundations for the church, the needs of individuals, the framework of philosophy, and basic intentions are established, program and structure should emerge. Too often, structure is continued in the absence of an understood philosophical framework (the basic "why" of existence). Philosophical frameworks may change as understanding of roles and responsibilities change. Once the philosophical framework has changed, structure and programming should change to meet those needs.

The structure and programming provide the context and means by which the philosophical intents of the church are met. If the structure and programming are not meeting the intents of the church, the structure and programming may be changed to meet those intents. Perhaps, the issue and relationship may be clarified by remembering Jesus' words: "The sabbath was made for man, not man for the sabbath" (Mark 2:27). Thus, the structure and programming should not become an obstacle to be overcome. Rather, the structure and program should be ways of reaching the basic intents.

Structure and programming should reflect and flow naturally from the intent. For example, if the church's intent involves the democratic participation of all members in decision making, then a nonparticipative form of church government or practice reflects incongruency. Such tension does not promote growth toward intent; rather, it promotes perpetuation of an unstated or hidden agenda.

In conclusion, the basic thrust of the church is to teach and to reach out to others. In fact, Christian education must involve outreach by its very core. If Christian education is assisting individuals to find and to grow in their proper relationship to God, self, and fellow human beings, then outreach is essential. As lives are changed, a missionary nature of outreach is automatic. To teach demands the task of reaching out.

The three basic institutions of Christian education have been described in light of their purpose and distinctive qualities. Many institutions exist today. We have numerous families that are not Christian; we have various schools both private and public that are not Christian schools; we have clubs and other organizations that are not churches. What makes the Christian family, the school, and the church different from any other family, school, or religious group? The answer lies in the context of relationships. The Christian institution recognizes the divine creation of human beings, the worth of the individual, the importance of community, and the relationship of God for both the individual as well as the corporate life. Relationship makes the difference.

Because humanity is created for relationship by a relational God, only in living in relation to Him can we find life. The same material may be studied or the same disciplinary techniques used in both Christian and non-Christian education. However, the relationship is of a special quality. Christian education provides the context where we may find abundant life. Scripture demonstrates that promise of relationship for those in Christian education: "For where two or three are gathered in my name, there am I in the midst of them" (Matt. 18:20).

Learning Activity 6.3

1. List various New Testament words that describe the church. What are the implications of these terms for Christian education?
2. Analyze the various programs of your church. Describe the basic purpose of each organization. How do you evaluate its effectiveness in reaching its stated purpose?
3. Survey various church members to determine what are their ideas of the church.
4. Ask nonchurch members to share their ideas of what the church is.
5. What message does your church teach in regard to how it acts through its various meetings and programs?

Distinctive Relational Qualities: The Model of the Shema

The Book of Deuteronomy provides an excellent portrait of the importance of educating or instructing in the way of the Lord. The Shema (Deut. 6:4-9) provides insight into how the Hebrews have been able to maintain their religious identity for thousands of years. Moses had led the children of Israel through varied experiences in the wilderness. At last they were preparing to enter the promised land. In going into a new land filled with pagan influences, they needed the message of the Shema. As Christians going into a non-Christian world, we need the message of the Shema in our families, schools, and churches. The Shema provides an excellent working model in guiding Christian education distinctives:

Hear, O Israel: The Lord our God is one Lord; and you shall love the
Lord your God with all your heart, and with all your soul, and with all
your might. And these words which I command you this day shall be
upon your heart; and you shall teach them diligently to your children,
and shall talk of them when you sit in your house, and when you walk
by the way, and when you lie down, and when you rise. And you shall
bind them as a sign upon your hand, and they shall be as frontlets between your eyes. And you shall write them on the doorposts of your
house and on your gates (Deut.6: 4-9).

Hear

Hear, O Israel: The Lord our God is one Lord (v. 4).

1. *Christian Education Acknowledges Its Primary Relationships.*—
We live in a pluralistic society, as did the Hebrews. There are many
supposed gods and goddesses—youth, sex, pleasure, power, and mate-
rialism. There are many who confuse us by claiming that all religions
lead to the same place. There are groups who speak of noble ideas or
truths, yet they do not profess the one Lord. Each of these "gods"
tries, both overtly and covertly, to direct our lives.

It is not possible to live in the world without relationships. Relationships form the fabric of our identity and behavior. Those who profess no religion and claim no relationship to God, in fact, possess a
relationship. Perhaps money is the one priority to which they relate.
All of life may be consumed and directed toward either the accumu-
lating or the spending of money. Perhaps the relationship is family. If
family is the center of relationships, then life revolves around the persons and issues of family.

We will inescapably choose a relationship with which to identify.
The Jews have been able to maintain their identity as family and as a
people for thousands of years. Other groups have appeared on the
scene quickly and have vanished just as quickly. Jews have maintained their identity. One reason may be found in this verse. In the
midst of a diversity of religions and religious practices, they were able

to say, "The Lord our God is one." Their identity with God both separated them and maintained them.

Today Christian families, schools, and churches need to know in whom they believe. We need to know with whom we are going to have relationship. Once we have decided whom we will believe and to whom we will relate, the rest of our lives will take on a new dimension. This type of acknowledgment sets the foundation for all new relationships. We must know whom and what we believe. All three—the family, the school, and the church—reflect relationships. The Christian family, school, and church acknowledge the Lord as one. From that priority of relationships all other relationships find their proper place. How we live, how we love, how we react to adversity, and how we react to prosperity are reflections of what we choose as our highest relationship.

2. Christian Education Involves a Place of Hearing God's Word.— This initial verse involves the importance of hearing. Hearing implies listening. For one to hear, one must listen. There are numerous voices to which our ears are drawn. Many messages exist which would lead and direct our behavior. Once we know the relationship which will have priority, we should direct our ears toward listening to its message. When a mother brings home her newborn baby, she becomes highly sensitive to the child's voice. At night mothers can hear their babies cry long before fathers do. Mothers can discern the voice of their child in the midst of a room of screaming babies. Mothers can differentiate between the different cries of their own children. One cry means "I'm wet." Another cry means "I'm lonely." Still another cry means "I'm hungry."

Churches, families, and schools need to develop such "motherly" sensitivity to God in their relationships. Such sensitivity can not be acquired magically nor automatically. Rather, the sensitivity and the hearing emerge from placing ourselves in a position to listen. Time must be spent in discerning the messages and voices of God. Many voices would seek to lead us. We must ask: To which voice will we listen? That one will form the highest priority of relationship.

3. Christian Education Acknowledges that We Are Not Alone.—In acknowledging that the Lord our God is one Lord, we acknowledge we are not alone. We are a part of something much greater than ourselves. We no longer have to search for relationship. We have fellowship. We have brothers and sisters in the Christian family, school, and church. While we are each different in our giftedness, we possess a unity that is uncharacteristic of other groups. We all serve the one true Lord. As fellow servants, we work, we rejoice, and we suffer together. In Christian education, we are no longer alone. The growth of one Christian learner enriches both individual and corporate growth and development. While we each possess our own responsibilities, we live together in responsible relationship to each other.

Love

> You shall love the Lord your God with all your heart, and with all your soul, and with all your might (v. 5).

4. Christian Education Teaches Obedient Love to God.—To whatever and whomever we decide to relate in life, our lives change and reflect that relationship. This command to love flows out of the acknowledgment of the Lord our God. The love described here is not one of mere warm sentiment as we might display toward another human being. Instead, this love involves reverence, devotion, and holy fear. Love of God requires obedience that grows. Love demands as the Scripture indicates: heart, soul, and might. Love of God without obedience is not love (1 John 4:7-21). The whole being is required in this obedient love relationship.

5. Christian Education Instills New Identity.—Relationships lead to our identity as persons. As we demonstrate love to God, we discover a new identity. For example, youth may relate to a particular group of friends. They may adopt the dress, the language, and the behavior of the group. Through the process of relating to others, youth establish their own sense of identity. Identity involves both the individual as well as the group.

For the Christian, in relationship and obedience to God, one finds identity. Christian education seeks to have each individual discover his or her own identity in Christ through personal relationship. We know whom we believe, and we obey Him: we have our identity. Identity and responsibility are mutually influencing. Luke 14:27 states, "Whoever does not bear his own cross and come after me, cannot be my disciple." All of humankind is seeking an identity—individuals, minority groups, or nations. True identity can only be found as obedient love to Christ is demonstrated.

Learning Activity 6.4

1. What relationships should Christian education seek to promote?
2. Do you agree or disagree with the statement, "Identity is made up of relationships"? Explain.
3. What relationships have your Christian education experiences sought to promote?

6. Christian Education Focuses Upon the Role of Modeling.— Christian education has the responsibility to help its members discover their own identities and how this identity corresponds into the overall scheme of life. All three educational institutions seek to lead their members to live mature lives. The family, school, and church are distinctive in their attempts to help members find their mature identity. In addition to providing basic skills, Christian education provides a value system with which to identify. Showing others how to live life involves modeling that life.

To show others how to meet the challenges and questions of life, mature members must take seriously the command to love God. As we model love and obedience to God, we show others how they can make decisions and face life's challenges. Once the primary relationship is established with love and obedience to God, we are in the best possible position to make the choices of life. It is unrealistic to expect obedience from others if we ourselves are disobedient.

Much of who we are and the identities we achieve result from our choice of models. Often the concept of "value free" teaching or "value free" counseling is expressed as a desired situation. However, such a concept does not exist. To decide not to have a value is to choose that particular value. Teachers teach more than just academic subject matter. Teachers teach their own values and live out of their own presuppositions. Learners, whether in kindergarten or in graduate school, are influenced by such modeling.

Discrimination must be practiced in selecting teachers who are going to be involved in the Christian education process. In addition, individuals must come to an awareness of the values they represent, both expressed and unexpressed. Nevertheless, while individuals should have freedom of teaching, responsibility exists to the value system they represent. Throughout the Christian educational system, behaviors should be practiced which model the Son of God.

7. Christian Education Provides Opportunities for Developing Service.—As we mature, there is an opportunity to grow in our love of God and its subsequent implications. A valid question is: Are we demonstrating a more obedient spirit and service to God today than we did yesterday? Both love and obedience are progressive. Both require opportunities for demonstration. Parents, as well as children, should be more obedient and loving as they grow older. What about your service to God? Has your obedience matured as you have increased in your ability to serve? What about to your family? Do you allow your family to mature in faith and practice?

The church, like the family and school, should mature in love and service to God. One measurement of assessing mature growth is to examine the life of the individual members. Are we better stewards of our time and financial resources today than we were yesterday? Are we more loving and forgiving today than we were yesterday? Are we more involved in the mission of the church today than we were yesterday? If so, we are maturing. If not, we are stagnating or dying. Christian education must provide opportunities for growth and service.

Learning Activity 6.5

1. What images are currently being modeled by Christians through the media?
2. What are some appropriate areas of service that Christian education should promote?
3. Schools are often identified by their graduates. Describe the "ideal graduate" of Christian education.

Teach

> These words, which I command you this day shall be upon your heart; and you shall teach them diligently to your children, and shall talk of them when you sit in your house, and when you walk by the way, and when you lie down, and when you rise (vv. 6-7).

8. Christian Education Involves All Its Members in Continued Instruction.—These words refer to God's revelation, teachings, and Commandments. We are first instructed to keep God's commands in our hearts; we are to keep His commandments in our living. Next we are commanded to teach what we know. One of the most difficult things to teach is what you do not know or do not fully or even adequately understand. As a teacher, I have often felt the pain of not knowing how to communicate information that I did not fully understand. However, the teaching described here should be a natural outpouring of what is already in the life and heart of the individual. This teaching is possible because one has already decided, acknowledged, and acted obediently to the Lord our God.

The verses demonstrate the importance of teaching children in the faith. Anytime our educational institutions fail to teach God's truth, we have a responsibility to act. Parents are often stirred to action if the school system fails to instruct their children adequately in the basic academic skills. However, do parents exert the same concern if the church fails to instruct its children in the Christian faith? By the same token, is the church concerned if its individual families fail to instruct their children properly in the Christian faith?

The church, as well as individual families and schools, has the responsibility to teach its children. Children of all ages come to church. No age is too young or old to hear and feel God's love.

The responsibility of teaching does not cease with a particular age. Just as there is a need for continual love and obedience, there is a need for continual teaching. Some of those reading this work may believe they are not teachers. Either formally or informally, we are all teachers. Either as a parent or as a Christian, we influence the character of those with whom we associate.

The Shema illustrates the importance of teaching and explaining the faith in our daily lives. We do not teach apart from our daily lives. We teach in our daily lives, our daily activities, and our daily habits. Being a follower of Christ and being a Christian parent is a twenty-four-hour task each day. Being a Christian means that our lives are intertwined with the lives of others. We do not have an escape from relationships. Rather, being a Christian allows us to relate to people in love because of our having a love relationship with God Himself.

In the church, as well as in the family and school, we teach a message about God and about ourselves. Each age and each movement in life provides an opportunity for teaching and learning. Even before the birth of the child, the church and family have an important role in ministering to the unborn child by caring for and preparing the expectant parents. As the child progresses through various life stages, opportunities exist for the church to teach: presenting the child with a first Bible, providing the child with quality Bible teaching opportunities, and planning various activities for growth. During adolescence, the church and family have obligations to teach youth about sexual morality, conduct, knowing God's will, and selecting a mate. During the adult years, the church has the responsibility to teach how to live life more faithfully. Even in death, and how we approach the event, we teach a message.

The totality of life provides opportunities to teach what is in our hearts. Life, faith, and teaching cannot be compartmentalized. Faith requires life-span obedience, devotion, and instruction.

For the teacher, in either a lay religious program or a private college, it must be emphasized that teaching extends beyond the confines of an hour on Sunday. Teaching extends beyond the classroom into the life context of the individual. Informal settings can often provide as many teaching opportunities as formal meetings. Teachable moments cannot always be planned on the academic or curricular schedule.

Obey

> You shall bind them as a sign upon your hand, and they shall be as frontlets between your eyes. And you shall write them on the doorposts of your house and on your gates (vv. 8-9).

9. Christian Education Chooses Appropriate Behaviors to Convey Its Message.—These symbols and rituals were to instruct the family, as well as the community, of the special difference in lives brought about by faith in God. Symbols and rituals are important for the family, school, and church. It may be advantageous to describe rituals as organized patterns of behavior or organized ways of providing witnesses to our relationships. It involves a means of preserving and passing on the faith. However, a danger exists if we use symbols and rituals without knowing the meaning behind the ritual or symbol. Rituals or patterns of behavior such as Bible reading, praying, witnessing, and giving are important in the life of the church and believer.

When the ritual become ritualization and the acts are devoid of their intended meaning, we have lost our focus. What do you do in your daily life? Is it ritual or ritualistic? Going to public worship, giving of tithe and offerings, and teaching Sunday School are each opportunities for genuine meaning. However, we may go through these activities without having or knowing the purpose in mind.

For example, why do you attend Sunday School? Why does the church operate a Sunday School? A Sunday School exists not because we have always had one. At least, it should not exist for that reason. Rather, the Sunday School exists for the purpose of teaching biblical revelation and for outreach. If your Sunday School functions but is not reaching out and growing, then there may be something missing. The Sunday School, like other program organizations of the church, exists for the purpose of the church's mission. Stagnation is not possible if one is on mission. Either the Sunday School or church is on mission or is in need of a mission.

Family practices of worship and behavior should reflect a living relationship. Activities are important if they truly reflect the intended spirit. The Jewish people were proficient in their rituals and in their organized ways of sacrifice. Unfortunately, the act of devotion became divorced from the spirit or the meaning. Many passages of Scripture illustrate this condition. Hosea 6:6 states: "For I desire steadfast love and not sacrifice,/the knowledge of God, rather than burnt offerings." Proverbs 21:3 states: "To do righteousness and justice/is more acceptable to the Lord than sacrifice." The problem was not in the sacrifice itself or the act of worship: the problem was the lack of meaning or intent of the worship.

To maintain identity as a Christian family, school, or church, we should seek to establish those practices that will allow us to worship God and to witness for God. Because of our relationship with Him, our very way of living life should be different. Life should remind us of God's love and our need to witness that love to others. Family customs and church practices should seek to remind us of the unity in Christ that we share.

In formal Christian schooling, appropriate symbols and behaviors must be chosen carefully. What we do is important. Care must be taken that we do not adopt the attitude and the practice of the Pharisees. In their attempts to keep the "letter of the law," the Pharisees adopted a host of laws to ensure the keeping of the letter of the law. However, in keeping the letter of the law, the spirit of the law may be lost. On occasion, the form may be maintained but the essence of meaning lost.

Whatever we do should reflect our own Christian commitments and value beliefs. Analysis and reflection are important. We will not always know immediately what to do. Revision is necessary. Christian education must choose behaviors that demonstrate its highest ideals and hopes.

Learning Activity 6.6

1. What are some typical Christian educational experiences in which you engage? Include the formal as well as the informal.
2. Describe some teachable moments in the Christian faith that were unplanned but important to you.
3. Paraphrase Deuteronomy 6:8-9.
4. What is the relationship between symbols and meanings?
5. What should guide individuals as they seek appropriate symbols and behaviors for Christian education?

Conclusions on Our Distinctiveness

The most significant conclusion about Christian education resides in its power and authority. In His parting words to His disciples, Jesus said, "All authority in heaven and on earth has been given to me. Go therefore and make disciples of all nations, baptizing them in the name of the Father and of the Son and of the Holy Spirit, teaching them to observe all that I have commanded you; and lo, I am with you always, to the close of the age" (Matt. 28:18-20).

10. Christian Education Has Divinely Given Power.—Unlike other groups, the Christian family, school, and church possess a power that no one else possesses. Jesus has promised the presence of His Holy Spirit to guide us as we go to make disciples. The family, the school, and the church are involved in discipleship. No power can match that power given to those who believe in the only begotten Son of God. Jesus promises that the "powers of death shall not prevail against it [the church]" (Matt. 16:18). The church will ultimately be victorious in life. Such victory is shared by the quest for Christian education if it seeks to follow the mandate to go and "make disciples."

The Christian is one who has accepted a special relationship to God through faith in Jesus Christ. Christians, whether in the church, the family, the school, or the business world, have the task of helping others find that special relationship by their witness. The conviction of sin and turning in repentance are works of the Holy Spirit. Our task is to witness. As we faithfully witness, we nurture that identity of relationship to God.

We often engage in extensive missionary activities around the world. However, we fail to take the mission imperative to our own families, church, and schools. What we do not share, we lose. The Christian faith, whether it be in the home, church, or school, if not shared, may be lost.

Whether we wish it so or not, history repeats itself. Today we are modeling a role of family, the school, and the church for the next generation. Equally as true, we are in the process of modeling for all future generations. The idea is a sobering thought. The hope lies in personal faith and obedience to Jesus Christ and witnessing to others.

The Christian family, church, and school will maintain their identity to the extent that they practice their faith. Many gods and goddesses today call us to worship them. Sometimes the appeal is very obvious, and sometimes it is very subtle. We maintain our identities by remembering the Lord our God is one. Out of that acknowledgment should flow obedient love, witness, growth, and behavior. Jesus has been given all authority, and He has promised to be with us. We will exist and flourish as long as we cherish and practice the distinctive nature of our call.

Learning Activity 6.7

1. What are the strengths of Christian education as reflected in the family, school, and church? What are its weaknesses as currently practiced?
2. Will the family, school, and church maintain their distinctive qualities? Explain.

Notes

1. Lester A. Kirkendall and Arthur E. Gravatt, *Marriage and the Family in the Year 2020* (Buffalo, New York: Prometheus Books, 1984), 13-14.

2. John W. Drakeford, *This Insanity Called Love* (Waco, Tex.: Word Books, 1970), 142-45.

3. Kirkendall and Gravatt, 15-18.

4. Ibid., 18-22.

5. Ben C. Fisher, "The Case for the Christian College," *Adult Leadership*, February 1976, 10-11.

6. Robert A. Baker, *Tell the Generations Following: A History of the Southwestern Baptist Theological Seminary 1908-1983* (Nashville: Broadman Press, 1983), 182.

7. Herschel H. Hobbs, *The Baptist Faith and Message* (Nashville: Convention Press, 1971), 75.

8. Howard P. Colson and Raymond M. Rigdon, *Understanding Your Church's Curriculum*, rev. ed. (Nashville: Broadman Press, 1981), 35.

7
Christian Education Revealed in Stewardship

An Overview of the Relationship Theme

Throughout this work, the importance of relationships in Christian education has been emphasized. Christian education should seek to aid persons to find, experience, and enjoy their relationship to God through Christ. Out of relationship to Christ, human beings acquire a stewardship orientation. Stewardship and discipleship are parallel expressions of a relationship with God. Stewardship impacts the four basic relationships in which human beings find themselves involved: God, self, others, and the world. Each influences the others.

Stewardship involves a world view, a philosophy in which human beings demonstrate responsible living in the world. Stewardship is commanded from the beginning of biblical revelation. In the Genesis account (1:28), humans were to exercise dominion over the earth. Unfortunately, because of human rebellion, the relationship changed. Rather than humanity's exercising dominion over the earth, the earth has dominion over humanity. Through their own neglect, human beings have abused their relationship to the earth. Other relationships are equally distorted.

Old Testament Viewpoint

In the Old Testament, the steward is not the owner; the steward is the manager or the trustee. The Old Testament gives a clear picture of God's ownership of the world, an ownership that exists in light of God's creation of the world.

The world belongs to God. He said to man, "Be fruitful and multiply, and fill the earth and subdue it; and have dominion over the fish of the sea and over the birds of the air and over every living thing that moves upon the earth" (Gen. 1:28). Created in the image of God, humanity was to exercise control over the world. Control did not involve exploitation or abuse but implied nurturance. Human dominion or control over the world was to be one of nurturing care.

Another illustration of human stewardship concerns the tithe. Various references throughout the Old Testament pertain to the tithe. One tenth of the increase in grain, fruit, cattle, and sheep were to be given to the Levites and the priests each year. This symbol reminded the Israelites that the land belonged to the Lord, and the increase was God's gift.[1]

New Testament Viewpoint

Various words in the New Testament illustrate the concept of stewardship. Stewardship is a broad concept that includes responsibility for all that human beings possesses: material possessions, experiences, and relationships. William Hendricks analyzes three aspects of stewardship: substance, sanctification, and motivation.[2] Stewardship concerns the substances of life such as food, water, clothing, material goods, time, and the physical environment. It also involves the process of sanctification, Christian growth, and maturation. Involved with this stewardship of sanctification are self, the body of Christ, and society. In addition, a New Testament understanding of stewardship involves the concept of motivation. Hendricks writes, "The motive behind human stewardship is, in the last analysis, recognition of the divine stewardship to man in the redemption which is ours in Christ."[3]

Building upon the Old Testament, the New Testament stresses that stewardship and following God are intricately related. As God has sacrificially given so that we might have eternal life, we must give our life in a sacrificial life-style. All aspects of our relationships are to be given in stewardship. Stewardship is not so much something we do as it is who we are.

In order to begin to comprehend the complex nature of stewardship, focus will now be given to the four relationship directions in
which humanity is involved. While discussion is centered in each of
these four areas, it must be remembered that each area influences the
others. To be properly related to Christ involves the awareness that
what we do in one area affects all other areas. Relationships in one
aspect influence all of life's relationships. (See Figure 7.1).

Relationship to God

Only those who have professed faith in God through Christ have
the possibility for proper stewardship. Only in relationship with God
can human beings discover the significance of their behavior to other
relationships.

Priority to a Personal Relationship.—Four of the Ten Commandments (Ex. 20:1-17) stress humanity's relationship to God. The first
two Commandments demand that we have no other gods before God
and that we not make any graven images. To worship anyone or anything other than God signifies idolatry. Biblically, graven images
could refer to the various pagan images that were present in their
polytheistic world. In the twentieth century, graven images still exist;
however the forms have changed. Rather than ancient idols made of
wood or stone, modern idols may consist of steel in the form of an
automobile, brick and cement in the form of large homes with swim-
ming pools, and paper in the form of money, stocks, or bonds. Idolatry happens anytime we place higher priority on some entity than it
warrants.

Scripture clearly teaches that judgment and destruction will come
to those who forsake God and worship idols. Christian stewardship
allows us to forsake this type of idolatry. In stewardship, everything is
seen as belonging to God. Care and consideration are given to what
God has placed in our charge for a short period of time. Stewardship
shows us how to live our lives in proper relationship to God, ourselves, other people, and the world. Our most prized possession—our
priority—is our relationship to God.

RELATIONSHIPS OF STEWARDSHIP

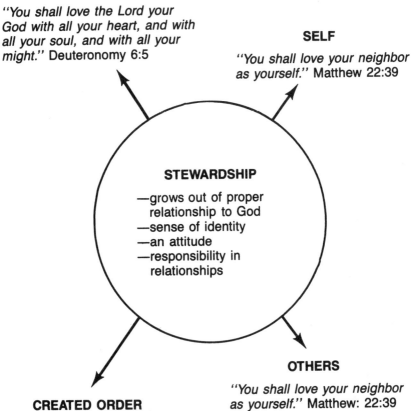

GOD

"You shall love the Lord your God with all your heart, and with all your soul, and with all your might." Deuteronomy 6:5

SELF

"You shall love your neighbor as yourself." Matthew 22:39

STEWARDSHIP

—grows out of proper relationship to God
—sense of identity
—an attitude
—responsibility in relationships

CREATED ORDER

"Be fruitful and multiply, and fill the earth and subdue it; and have dominion over the fish of the sea and over the birds of the air and over every living thing that moves upon the earth." Genesis 1:28

OTHERS

"You shall love your neighbor as yourself." Matthew: 22:39

"But let justice roll down like waters, and righteousness like an ever-flowing stream." Amos 5:24

Figure 7.1

Priority to the Community of Faith.—A part of our relationship to God involves our identification with the body of Christ or the community of faith. Our relationship with other believers is an important outgrowth of our Christian lives. We have basic need for fellowship with other believers and to be identified with a place for the worship of God.

The Old Testament records the importance of this involvement with God's people in a place of worship and service. One of the great moments in Jewish history occurred in 586 B.C. with Nebuchadnezzar's capture of Jerusalem. With Jerusalem destroyed, the Jews were deported to Babylonia where they lived under Babylonian rule. In 539 B.C., Cyrus of Persia captured Babylonia and permitted the Jews to return to Jerusalem.

The Jewish temple, which had been destroyed by Nebuchadnezzar in 586 B.C., still lay in ruins, with only the stone foundations remaining. During the previous seventy years, those people left behind had become accustomed to worshiping in the remains of the old temple. Perhaps their vision of God had also vanished.

In this setting, the Lord called the prophet Haggai to minister God's Word to His people. While the people might argue that times were economically difficult and not convenient to the building of the temple, Haggai saw their difficulty as a reflection of their lack of concern for and obedience to the will of God. Although times were difficult, the people had nevertheless built their own homes to the neglect of the temple.

Continued indifference toward God would contribute to their own misfortune. Haggai's concern was not merely for a physical building but for a type of orientation that would give the presence of God first place. Rebuilding the temple was a way of putting God first in a "concrete" fashion. Human nature requires a place where we can find meaning and reality for living. For Haggai, that center was the place where God would choose to make His presence known. If the people would work toward building God's temple, then God would bless them. The people listened and responded. Four years after Haggai had made his appeal, the temple was completed in 516 B.C.

It would be unfortunate to consider the building of God's temple to reflect only physical structures. Rather, the Christian has a unique opportunity "to build the temple" in a way that exceeds mere physical structure. "Building the temple" involves acts of redemption—the ministering of the Word to a lost and dying world. "Building the temple" today means opportunities: preaching the Word to those in all parts of the world, both home and abroad; healing the sick and comforting the dying; educating individuals in the ways of God from a local church level to the highest levels of graduate education; and strengthening and rebuilding families. The possibilities for ministry grow larger and larger. All of these opportunities require the giving of ourselves, not only in financial resources but also in talent and time.

Like the people of Haggai's day, we focus on our own wants and desires to the neglect of God's temple—His mission. Research reveals that approximately 20 percent of the church membership supports 80 percent of the church's financial responsibility. We focus on building our own "temples"—that may consist of homes, second homes, numerous cars, expensive clothes, vacations, and high-quality education. We omit service to God.

Today we live in hard-pressed economic times. However, God's temple is to be built both in days of prosperity as well as days of adversity. Investing in the work of God involves investing in the eternal and not the temporal. Real-estate investments may rise and fall; investments in God's Word never fail. Isaiah 40:8 states:

> The grass withers, the flower fades;
> but the word of our God will stand forever.

The guiding purpose of stewardship finds expression within the church as well as the individual life. Matthew 16:18 states, "I tell you, you are Peter, and on this rock I will build my church, and the powers of death shall not prevail against it." The rock refers to the acknowledged faith or the confessions of the disciple to the lordship of Christ. Acknowledged faith can only find substance as it involves the life of stewardship. Words without complementary actions are meaningless.

The great moments in church history reveal both individuals and churches who give themselves sacrificially to the work of God. Relating to Christ involves relating to His Church.

Priority of Faith Proclamation and Ministry.—Another significant aspect of our lives in regard to the body of Christ concerns the importance of our own profession of faith with its accompanying responsibilities and privileges. A clear example is found in Peter's declaration or confession in Matthew 16:13-20. Jesus responded to Peter's declaration of Him as the Christ by saying that upon this type of faith, He would build His church. The keys of the kingdom are given to those of the faith. The keys of the kingdom may refer to the faith. As we proclaim our faith, we are showing others the way to God. Faith must be declared.

Declared Faith Involves Authority.—In the Great Commission (Matt. 28:18-20), Jesus said "All authority . . . has been given to me." As His disciples, authority is given to us. In fact, Jesus said that His disciples would do works far greater than He had done (John 14:12). Power and authority are given to those who declare their faith in Christ.

We possess different types of gifts; each gift is an opportunity of service. The gift will unlock certain doors of faith witnessing; some doors it will not. Each of us has a different gift from God. While the gift is individual, it is given for benefit of community. Our gifts are privileges or opportunities through which we can witness to others. Gifts enable us to release a treasure into the world. Gifts are opportunities of unlocking doors of ministry to the world.

Christian education should help the persons to discover their own giftedness. Discovering and developing giftedness must be done in relationship to the work of the Kingdom. Our gifts are for service and ministry.

Relationship to Self

What relationship is one to have to self? When asked what is the greatest commandment, Jesus replied: "You shall love the Lord your

God with all your heart, and with all your soul, and with all your mind. This is the great and first commandment. And a second is like it, You shall love your neighbor as yourself. On these two commandments depend all the law and the prophets" (Matt. 22:37-40). We are commanded to love ourselves. This type of love does not entail narcissism—a type of self-absorption. Rather, this love is a healthy and mature love that recognizes all of life's basic needs and how the individual life is to be involved in those relationships. To truly love myself involves worshiping God and demonstrating high ethical concern for those around me. In the biblical view, loving oneself is a healthy experience, one to be treasured. If we love ourselves, we will seek those relationships and a life-style that will bring us eternal fulfillment and joy.

Individually, our personalities may carry scars from experiences over which our control may be minimal or nonexistent. Child abuse, disappointment, lack of love, and insecurity typically affect our present lives. Even Christians often display emotional or psychological scars. Even now, we may be engaging in self-defeating behaviors. Often the things we claim to want intensely, we deny by our own actions. We may be hurting ourselves with needless self-criticism and self-defeating behaviors. We may fail to love ourselves in the biblically required fashion.

In these very areas of life—our deep emotional scars, our self-defeating behaviors and attitudes—we have the responsibility to exercise our God-given stewardship. Often lives are lived in such a way that the person is no longer in control. Pain, hurt, and anguish control the person. A Christian view of stewardship involves assuming responsibility for our lives. While our responsibility in the past may be minimal, we are responsible for the present moment in which we live. In stewardship, we are held accountable for the lives we lead. Because God loves us, we are set free to love ourselves, as well as others.

To fail to love ourselves biblically is to deny a significant aspect of stewardship. To love ourselves involves a multitude of ideas. We must stop behaviors that are self-destructive. We must carefully evaluate all of our relationships to others, to material possessions, and to the world. Through the work of the Holy Spirit, we can discover how we can positively love ourselves in a way pleasing to Christ.

We must also assume responsibility for who we are and who we will become. Some individuals constantly search for something they do not appear to find. Thoreau wrote of those who lead lives of quiet desperation. Some plans do not seem to work; we may never find that for which we are searching; we may never be satisfied. What can keep us from experiencing such desperation?

One reason for dissatisfaction or desperation is the failure to decide who we are and to assess the value of that decision. Good writing has a guiding purpose or thesis. This thesis directs all elements of the composition. It guides what is acceptable and nonacceptable to the proving of the thesis. It keeps the writer on target, avoiding extraneous material. Human lives require a thesis or guiding purpose.

The question of life-thesis is addressed again and again in biblical revelation: "Whom will you serve?" Individuals long for a thread to make the fabric of life meaningful, purposeful, and durable. Individuals need a standard by which to make choices. We are in the process of building individual lives, building homes, and building businesses, etc. In building anything, one must have a master plan or a guiding purpose.

For Christians, the guiding purpose should be the new identity in Christ. A basic principle from psychology states that whatever we think of ourselves (our self-concepts) will reflect in behavior. Deciding who we are is one of life's most significant questions. We owe it to ourselves to give the needed time and energy to find an answer to that question. When decided, our energies should be directed toward that goal.

Christian education can help us discover who we are and how we are to live. We may learn to think of ourselves as stewards. If I think of myself as a steward, I will be a steward. I can't help but be a steward. If stewardship is not a part of my identity in Christ, I cannot be one. Stewardship is an attitude that is expressed in action. Stewardship involves a recognition that all we have belongs to God (time, talents, and money), and that all we have is to be applied to His kingdom's work. In acknowledging ourselves as Christians, we acknowledge that God has lordship (ownership) of our lives. We do His bidding.

Whatever our degree of giftedness, we are responsible for the utilization of our talents, time, and other resources. The individual talents that we possess will often open new opportunities and experiences that are closed to other individuals. Individual talent, whether it be athletic, academic, artistic, or social, provides a unique opportunity for sharing the secrets and the mysteries of the kingdom of God. Perhaps the clearest example of this truth may be found in the life of Esther.

In a plot to destroy the Jewish exiles, Haman persuaded King Ahasuerus to issue a decree that all Jews were to be killed on a certain day. Esther, herself a Jew, was placed in a perilous position. The life of her people had to be balanced against her own safety and position. If she failed to speak to the king about the safety of her people, they might perish. If she spoke to the king, her own safety would be endangered. She alone was in a position to speak a word for her people. Her Uncle Mordecai spoke to her regarding the choice (Esth. 4:14), "Who knows whether you have not come to the kingdom for such a time as this?"

Such an outlook can invigorate our lives if we will examine our gifts—talents, opportunities, relationships, and experiences. After examination, we should ask how these gifts can be used for the Kingdom's work. Everyday moments take on eternal significance. Think of great missionaries such as William Carey and Adoniram Judson. What would have happened if they failed to use their gifts for God? The Bible states in Psalm 118:24, "This is the day which the Lord has made; let us rejoice and be glad in it." In using our gifts, we may discover that we have indeed been created for this very day.

Jesus often spoke in parables about the importance of using one's gift effectively. These parables illustrate the importance of using what is available and God's multiplying or honoring the attempt. When Jesus encountered the young boy with the five loaves and two fishes, He demonstrated the importance of utilizing what we have. Jesus took the boy's lunch that he freely gave to Jesus, gave thanks for it, and shared it with those around. Regardless of how much or little we possess, we are accountable for how we use what we have been given. In using what we have, we find we have much more.

Christians are aware of their bodies as the temple of God. As the temple of God, we are responsible for how we live our lives. We must not abuse our bodies by unhealthy practices, and we must also positively live our lives in healthy practices. As Christians, we are being sanctified. What we do with our lives affects our sanctification, our stewardship. How we live our lives, spend our limited energies, and direct our behaviors are related to the holy lives we were created to live. Seeking after that which will promote our sanctification should be a natural outgrowth of our maturity.

Learning Activity 7.1

1. Define in your own words what Christian stewardship involves.
2. Survey the Bible to identify individuals who gave evidence of being a steward.
3. Does your stewardship change from year to year? If so, how?
4. List what you consider to be your most valuable possessions on one side of the page. On the other side of the page, examine how you give those things to God.
5. What opportunities of Christian witness have you been given? How can you use your gifts more effectively in the days ahead?

Relationship to Others

Humanity is created for community; community is created by humanity. Relationships to others are significant for human life. Human beings can engage in few behaviors that do not involve the actual or the imagined presence of others. Humans are social beings who find quality of life in relationships to fellow human beings. In the beginning, God created humans for companionship—with Him and others. However, the brotherly love for which the human race was created quickly vanished. The first brothers, Cain and Abel, were at odds with each other. Jealousy existed over their relationships with God. Jealous over God's favor of Abel's offering, Cain slew Abel. Disharmony and murder occurred because of jealousy, and a further disintegration of relationships between humans resulted.

The proper treatment of other humans is a dramatic theme in the gospel. Exploitation of others is condemned. History records that even the most religious were often guilty of exploiting the less fortunate. When this situation arose, God called forth the prophets to speak His Word. Regardless of how we ceremonially profess love and allegiance to God, we must still treat our fellow humans with justice and dignity. Amos 5:21-24 records:

I hate, I despise your feasts,
and I take no delight in your solemn assemblies.
Even though you offer me your
burnt offerings and cereal offerings,
I will not accept them,
and the peace offerings of your fatted beasts
I will not look upon.
Take away from me the noise of your songs:
to the melody of your harps I will not listen.
But let justice roll down like waters,
and righteousness like an ever-flowing stream.

Our relationships with others should be characterized by justice. The New Testament records:

Beloved, let us love one another; for love is of God, and he who loves is born of God and knows God. He who does not love does not know God; for God is love. In this the love of God was made manifest among us, that God sent his only Son into the world, so that we might live through him. In this is love, not that we love God but that he loved us and sent his Son to be the expiation for our sins. Beloved, if God so loved us, we also ought to love one another. No man has ever seen God; if we love one another, God abides in us and his love is perfected in us (1 John 4:7-12).

Our relationship to others should be an imitation of that relationship which God has extended to us. As we are loved and accepted by God, we should love and accept others. Previously, we discussed the importance of a therapeutic core (empathy, genuineness, trustworthiness, and the Holy Spirit) in the learning process. In dealing with others, we should allow this therapeutic core to bridge our relationships with them. Whether we are accepted or rejected, our responsibility is in extending the bridge. Once the bridge is extended, our goal should reflect concern for finding their identity in God's Word. Relationally, we should do whatever we can to foster and to nurture the giftedness of another. As we experience new life, we help another experience new life; another helps another experience new life. The Great Commission is fulfilled relationally as well as geographically.

Learning Activity 7.2

1. Respond to the statement, "Christians should love themselves."
2. What does love allow to occur in an individual's life? Is love an end in itself, or is love a means to something else?
3. What parts of speech describe Christian love? Explain.
4. Write a character sketch of someone who loves himself or herself in a negative fashion. Compare it with a sketch of someone who loves himself or herself in a biblical fashion.

Relationship to the Created Order

Stewardship, in the context of a right relationship with God, illustrates itself in right relationship with the rest of the created order. This viewpoint was evident to the Hebrew mind. Living in an agrarian society, the Hebrews knew well the importance of soil conservation and good treatment of the earthly resources. Pollution and wearing out the soil were forbidden.

As we look at our present society, we discover that these prohibitions are no longer followed. In fact, recent generations are noted for the ways in which they have sought to destroy the earth's resources with pollution and pesticides. We often live for today as though tomorrow will not exist. For the Hebrew, the present was vitally linked to the future.

Human beings not only have a responsibility for themselves but also for the future of their children. We often engage in a social trap. A social trap refers to a current situation in which we may be able to use resources to our fullest benefit, but in the process we may destroy the possible usage by future generations. We may be concerned only with our own benefits and not the benefits of society as a whole. Stewardship never involves only the self and the present moment; stewardship looks to others and to the future.

Conclusion

Our current view of stewardship has become dangerously microscopic in scope. We see stewardship as financial, rather than as a total and life-encompassing attitude. Today we learn from pulpits, television, radios, magazines, and newspapers that if we give financially to God we will receive financial rewards. That idea may or may not be true. Unfortunately, it may create a false image and practice in our lives. We may decide to give, thinking we will receive back more of what we gave. We may be treating God as though He were a stock market. We invest money in God's temple with the hope that rich material profits will follow.

Such a viewpoint and practice has questionable motivation. It is an unbiblical position. What the steward is promised is the presence of God in his or her life. If there is genuine stewardship, there is proper relationship with God. If there is proper relationship with God, there is genuine stewardship. In the presence of God, life begins to take on new meaning, stability, and direction. Being a steward of God is not limited to the church; stewardship reveals itself in the total life of the individual. If God is first, then decisions about all we have been given are made in light of His love and purpose.

As we practice our stewardship, let us not try to define exactly how God is going to bless. Let God define the relationship by His promise of being with us. As Jesus sent His disciples into the world to share the good news, He made them this promise: "All authority in heaven and on earth has been given to me. Go therefore and make disciples of all nations, baptizing them in the name of the Father and of the Son and of the Holy Spirit, teaching them to observe all that I have commanded you; and lo, I am with you always, to the close of the age" (Matt. 28:18-20). We are promised God's presence in our lives.

Stewardship is a life-style call that affects how we interact with God, ourselves, others, and the world. John Donne wrote "No man is an island." His thought applies to a biblical understanding of human beings. No relationship is done entirely unto itself. What is done in one area of life affects other areas of life. Individual life choices influence the life choices of others. Christian education addresses stewardship as it deals with the Christian faith. A tremendous opportunity and responsibility exists in carrying and passing on the faith to others. This concept is clearly demonstrated in the life of Paul and Timothy. Paul admonished Timothy about the importance of keeping the faith. Keeping the faith involves various dimensions. First, in one dimension keeping the faith reflects the need to remain faithful, throughout life and circumstance, to the faith that we have been taught. We should not abandon the faith either in times of adversity or times of prosperity. Second, keeping the faith involves the need to instruct and to pass on our faith to the next generation. On a third level, keeping the faith means keeping doctrinal purity. Often we experience the temptation to change or to alter the faith in keeping with our own tendencies or predispositions. In the process, we sometimes forget that the faith we possess belongs to God.

Christian education has a high privilege and responsibility in conveying faith to the world. Good stewardship is essential in the process of Christian education. Those involved in Christian education should commit themselves to a biblical understanding and practice. To be involved in solid Christian education requires a commitment and a price to be paid. As Christians, we are each involved in some level of Christian education. The process is not to be entered into lightly.

Learning Activity 7.3

1. Brainstorm reasons why we often feel disharmony or poor fellowship even in Christian groups. What are some solutions to this disharmony?
2. Respond to the statement, "One cannot have a proper vertical relationship with God if there is an improper horizontal relationship with one's neighbor." Use Scripture to support your position.
3. A social trap is using resources to our own fullest benefit in such a way that we may limit its usage potential for future generations. What are some of our social traps?
4. Are there such things as Christian social traps? Name them. How can we prevent such traps from occurring?
5. You have been asked to prepare a ninety-second commercial in which you present a biblical portrayal of stewardship. What would you include in your commercial? Why?

Notes

1. Ralph L. Smith, "Old Testament Concepts of Stewardship," *Southwestern Journal of Theology* 13 (Spring 1971): 12.

2. William L. Hendricks, "Stewardship in the New Testament," *Southwestern Journal of Theology* 13 (Spring 1971): 25-33.

3. Ibid., 33.

8
The Here and Now

An Overview of the Relationship Theme

Relationships form the core of our identity and our practice of Christian education. Living relationships must be constantly reviewed, revised, and recommitted. The process of Christian education is a dynamic one of growth and development in relationships. Christian education enables its participants to develop a Christian world view that aids in relating to the various dimensions of life. As we develop a Christian world view, specific plans are needed for planned growth in relationship living.

Relationship Learning acquaints the reader with the study of Christian education. Christian education is more than an involvement with a Sunday School lesson for forty minutes on a Sunday morning; Christian education is more than Bible study with friends in a home; Christian education is more than a weekend retreat from the hectic pace of life. While involving all of these examples, Christian education is much more encompassing. Based upon biblical and theological foundations, Christian education is a ministry of nurturing individuals in the Word so that life in Christ may be lived fully.

The concept *relationship* is familiar to the reader of this interpretation of Christian education. Basic to our lives is the relational emphasis. Created in the image of a relational God, we are born through the relationship of our parents. Once born, human beings begin their own struggle to find their own relational identity. Christian education provides guidance in this quest.

Throughout the text, numerous personal learning activities have been provided to encourage the readers to examine for themselves the nature and subsequent obligations of Christian education. The greatest challenge now resides with the reader. The reader has the responsibility of evaluating the work. More importantly, readers must decide their own involvement in the basic process. Before closing this interpretative investigation, several key assumptions need to be reinstated.

1. Each reader must think individually about the central issues raised in this work. Accept no statement without inquiry. Caring enough to question is the beginning of finding answers.

2. Christian education is not passive, not weak, not merely repetitive, and not strictly content. Christian education is actively relational.

3. While various aspects of Christian education have been explained rationally, the mystery cannot be dismissed. The Holy Spirit directs lives toward the Creator. While highly planned events may "appear" to succeed or fail, the Holy Spirit is still working a mystery within us.

4. Practices of Christian education have tended to reflect a cultural model. This observation has both positive and negative connotations. While educational practices must reflect the needs and the understanding levels of the target group, Christian education must not allow the culture to be the ultimate designer in terms of context, and content, and relationship. Rather, biblical standards must be discovered and then presented in a way that speaks to each new generation.

The process of Christian education must constantly undergo reinterpretation and revision by each generation of concerned Christians. The education we present will be the medium through which the voice and call of God may speak to the present and future generations.

5. Christian education is a lifelong process that demands active participation. All disciples are involved in Christian education as they live. The question is whether our involvement level is high or low.

Learning Activity 8.1

1. What is Christian education?
2. Has your concept of Christian education changed through reading this book? If so, in what ways?
3. What should be added to or deleted from this work to improve its usefulness as introductory study?
4. How valid is a "relational" approach to Christian education? Why?

The Need for a Model or World View

Whether it be the theologically trained minister or the layperson, each individual has a world view through which he or she perceives, judges, and makes behavioral decisions. We cannot escape having a model. The question is whether we have a model that is based upon clearly defined biblical principles or not. The readers are encouraged to examine the models by which they view and act in the world. We should each examine our model because the model guides our behavioral choices and our transmitting those choices. Christian education has the responsibility for assisting disciples to develop their world view or world model.

The "spectacle" or "eyeglass" model is a way of viewing the world and making behavioral choices. The "spectacles" refer to the eye wear of the individual. These spectacles represent the theological or biblical perspective that individual Christians must wear as they scrutinize the world. The spectacles provide theological meaning to the world under study. All of the world represents a part of God's truth. Humanity is free to study the created order in the attempt to have dominion over it in responsible stewardship. The world of science and the arts must be explored as they are a part of God's created order. Several assumptions are inherent within this model.

1. The lenses of the spectacles must be subject to review. The lenses may need to be changed or readjusted. This "readjustment" is necessary because the lenses of theological or biblical perspectives refer to

the individual's interpretations. Facts must not be confused with interpretations. Interpretations must be be subject to change.

2. The spectacles provide insight or vision for theological meaning and understanding. The spectacles are theological eyeglasses, not scientific eyeglasses. These spectacles reveal truth the individual alone is not equipped to discover.

3. As part of God's truth, all of the world is capable of being studied. Because human vision is limited and requires theological eyeglasses, complete truth or total meaning may not be possible for the present. At present, the spectacles are dim, but the future promises clearer vision.

4. The spectacles must be kept close to the individual inquirer. These spectacles provide the guiding purpose or ultimate direction for the searcher. Without some type of meaning, the individual may become lost in the maze of scientific investigation and humanistic speculation.

5. The best "frames" must be sought for the spectacles. The "frames" may represent the cultural values, the denomination, the institution, psychological or emotional barriers, or intellectual barriers that encase the theological lenses. The frames should allow the individual to have full use of theological lenses. The frames must be carefully chosen and adjusted when necessary. Care must be exercised lest the frames hinder the theological vision.

6. Each discipline studied must keep its projection within the scope of its observations and domain. Each discipline has certain limitations and assumptions from which it begins based on it own nature. For example, the field of mathematics should not project its findings into the biological sciences. We should not allow any discipline or study to assert what it cannot assert.

7. The "lenses" of the spectacles must be properly adjusted to the level of the individual. As the individual experiences growth and maturation, the lenses must experience the same. The more finely-developed mind must possess more finely-developed theological eyeglasses.

A Plan for Action

Throughout the text, various questions and activities have been designed to help the reader answer the important question: "So what?" Now that the material has been presented, what is the next direction for the reader? A plan of action is required (See Figures 8.1 and 8.2). These guidelines are offered:

1. Assume responsibility for developing a plan of education for yourself, your family, and your church.—A tragic mistake is to assume that someone else will direct your educational experience. The age of accountability refers to an age in which the individuals are responsible for their own lives in relationship to decisions regarding the call of Christ. Accountability also applies to the plan for growth and development in our lives. If you are able to read and to comprehend these words, you are accountable for your own plan of Christian education.

2. Develop a plan that is consistent with a biblical mandate.—This plan should include a thorough search of what is involved in growth in Christian maturity. Activities that help the individual to achieve the status of "accountable steward" are necessary.

3. Develop a plan that includes objectives and specific activities.— Do not drift into Christian education activities. Rather, plan the specifics. Discipline is required.

4. Develop a plan that includes both individual study and community participation.—The community alone cannot provide the basis for Christian growth and maturity; neither can the individual. The individual must not see his growth as separate from the greater community of faith. Enriched individual growth enriches the community; enriched community growth enriches the individual.

5. Remember the work of the Holy Spirit.—While stress has been placed on understanding the fundamental principles of Christian education and the need for specific plans to work toward, one truth remains. Individuals should not be so concerned with the plan that they forget the overall goal. If we are not careful, we may come to worship

"Relational" Bible Lesson /Study Plan

Passage: _____

Background Information: _____

_____

_____

_____

Related Passages: _____

_____

_____

_____

Life Characteristics and Needs of Learner: _____

_____

_____

_____

_____

Passage Meaning: What are the truths contained in the passage? __

_____

_____

Needs/Relationships: To which relationships or needs does this passage apply? What is the basic message?

_____

_____

Action: Based on my understanding, I shall engage in the following:

_____

_____

_____

Why/Motivation: What is the motivation for engaging in such action? What areas of my stewardship will be improved?

_____

_____

_____

Figure 8.1

Individualized Christian Education Development Plan

Assessment: Analyze your current needs (sensate, fellowship, competency, knowledge, and creativity): _____

_____

_____

_____

_____

_____

_____

Analyze your areas of relationships needs (God, self, others and created order): _____

_____

_____

_____

_____

_____

Action Plan: Based on my understanding of my needs and biblical truths, these are objectives for my own Christian education growth:

Objective:	Date	Resources Needed

_____

_____

_____

_____

_____

_____

_____

_____

_____

_____

_____

_____

_____

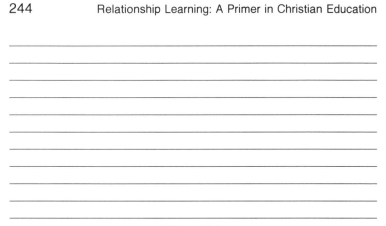

Figure 8.2

the creation and not the Creator. The Holy Spirit must provide the power to sustain and to allow us to grow in grace. In various ways through various lives, the Holy Spirit ultimately leads to new heights of Christian learning.

Learning Activity 8.2

1. What are your reactions to the "spectacle" or "eyeglass" model of viewing the world and making behavioral choices?
2. Create your own working model for viewing the world and making behavioral choices.
3. Design your own program of Christian enrichment experiences for the coming year. Break it down into months. Consult with your church in learning what opportunities are ahead for both corporate and individual growth.
4. What do you believe would be the most enriching Christian education experiences that you personally need?
5. Plan a balanced program of Christian education for your church.
6. What do you believe are the crucial elements in a Christian education program for every believer? Why?

Bibliography

Books

Baker, Robert A. *A Summary of Church History.* Nashville: Broadman Press, 1959.
_____ *Tell the Generations Following: A History of the Southwestern Baptist Theological Seminary 1908-1983.* Nashville: Broadman Press, 1983.

Barclay, William. *Educational Ideals in the Ancient World.* Grand Rapids: Baker Book House, 1959.

Bloom, B. S. et al. *Taxonomy of Educational Objectives: Handbook I, Cognitive Domain.* New York: D. McKay, 1956.

Butler, J. Donald. *Four Philosophies and Their Practice in Education and Religion,* 3d ed. New York: Harper & Row Publishers, 1968.

Callahan, Raymond E. *An Introduction to Education in American Society: A Text With Readings.* Foreword by George S. Counts. New York: Alfred A. Knopf, 1956.

Colson, Howard P. and Rigdon, Raymond M. *Understanding Your Church's Curriculum,* rev. ed. Nashville: Broadman Press, 1981.

Deaux, Kay and Wrightsman, Lawrence S. *Social Psychology in the 80s,* 4th ed. Monterey, California: Brooks-Cole Publishing, 1984.

Drakeford, John W. *This Insanity Called Love.* Waco, Tex.: Word Books, 1970.

Eavey, C. B. *History of Christian Education.* Chicago: Moody Press, 1964.

Eby, Frederick. *The Development of Modern Education: In Theory, Organization and Practice,* 2d ed. Englewood Cliffs, N.J.: Prentice-Hall, Inc., 1952.

Elton, G. R. *Reformation Europe: 1517-1559,* Fontana History of Europe. Edited by J. H. Plumb. Fontana, England: Collins, 1963.

Erikson, Erik H. *The Life Cycle Completed: A Review.* New York: W. W. Norton & Company, 1982.

Feist, Jess. *Theories of Personality.* New York: Holt, Rinehart and Winston, 1985.

Ford, LeRoy. *Design for Teaching and Training: A Self-Study Guide to Lesson Planning.* Nashville: Broadman Press, 1978.

Fowler, James S. *Stages of Faith: The Psychology of Human Development and the Quest for Meaning.* New York: Harper & Row, 1981.

Gaustad, Edwin Scott. *A Religious History of America.* New York: Harper & Row, 1966.

Good, H. G. *A History of Western Education*, 2d ed. New York: Macmillan Company, 1960.

Grant, Michael. *The History of Ancient Israel*. New York: Charles Scribner's Sons, 1984.

Gundry, Robert H. *A Survey of the New Testament*. Grand Rapids: Zondervan Press, 1970.

Gutek, Gerald L. *A History of the Western Educational Experience*. New York: Random House, 1972.

Harris, A. Christine. *Child Development*. Saint Paul: West Publishing Company, 1986.

Heichelheim, Fritz M.; Yes, Cedric A.; and Ward, Alfred M. *A History of the Roman People*, 2d ed. Englewood Cliffs, N.J.: Prentice-Hall Co., 1984.

Hester, H. I. *The Heart of Hebrew History: A Study of the Old Testament*. Liberty, Mo.: Quality Press, 1962.

Hirsch, E. D. *Cultural Literacy: What Every American Needs to Know*. Boston: Houghton Mifflin Co., 1987.

Hobbs, Herschel. *The Baptist Faith and Message*. Nashville: Convention Press, 1971.

Huyck, Margaret H., and Hoyer, William J. *Adult Development and Aging*. Belmont Calif.: Wadsworth Publishing Company, 1982.

Joy, Donald M., ed. *Moral Development Foundations: Judeo-Christian Alternatives to Piaget/Kohlberg*. Nashville: Abingdon Press, 1983.

Kirkendall, Lester A., and Gravatt, Arthur E. *Marriage and the Family in the Year 2020*. Buffalo, N. Y.: Prometheus Books, 1984.

Kagan, Donald; Ozment, Steven; and Turner, Frank M. *The Western Heritage*, 2d ed. New York: Macmillan Publishing Co., Inc., 1983.

Kienel, Paul. *The Christian School: Why It Is Right for Your Child*. Wheaton, Ill.: Victor Books, 1974.

Kohlberg, Lawrence. *Essays on Moral Development, Volume I: The Philosophy of Moral Development: Moral Stages, and the Idea of Justice* and *Volume II: The Psychology of Moral Development: The Nature and Validity of Moral Stages*. San Francisco: Harper & Row Publishers, 1981.

Krathwohl, D. R., et al. *Taxonomy of Educational Objectives: Handbook II. Affective Domain*. New York: D. McKay, 1964.

Lefrancois, Guy R. *Psychological Theories and Human Learning*, 2d ed. Monterey, Calif.: Brooks-Cole Publishing Co., 1982.

Leahey, Thomas Hardy. *A History of Psychology: Main Currents in Psychological Thought*, 2d ed. Englewood Cliffs, N.J.: Prentice-Hall, Inc., 1987.

Lynn, Robert W. and Wright, Elliott. *Big Little School: Two Hundred Years of Sunday School*, 2d ed. Birmingham: Religious Education Press, 1980.

Mayer, Frederick. *A History of Educational Thought*, 2d ed. Columbus, Ohio: Charles E. Merrill Books, Inc., 1966.

Meeks, Wayne A. *The First Urban Christians: The Social World of the Apostle Paul*. New Haven, Conn.: Yale University Press, 1983.

Monroe, Paul. *A Text-Book In The History of Education*. New York: Macmillan Co., 1905.

Monroe, Paul. *A Brief Course in the History of Education.* New York: Macmillan Co., 1907.

Oates, Wayne E. *The Psychology of Religion.* Waco, Tex.: Word Books, 1973.

Peters, Edward. *Europe and the Middle Ages.* Englewood Cliffs, N.J.: Prentice-Hall, Inc., 1983.

Price, J. M. *Jesus the Teacher.* Nashville: Convention Press, 1946.

Robinson, Daniel N. *An Intellectual History of Psychology.* Madison: The University of Wisconsin Press, 1986.

Santrock, John W. *Life-Span Development,* 2d and 3d ed. Dubuque, Iowa: Wm. C. Brown Co., Publishers, 1986 and 1989.

Schauss, Hayyim. *The Jewish Festivals: History and Observance.* Translated by Samuel Jaffe. New York: Schocken Books, 1938.

Schultz, Duane, and Schultz, Sydney Ellen. *A History of Modern Psychology,* 4th ed. New York: Harcourt Brace Jovanovich, Publishers, 1987.

Sherrill, Lewis J. *The Rise of Christian Education.* New York: The Macmillan Co., 1944.

Shurden, Walter, *The Doctrine of the Priesthood of the Believer.* Nashville: Convention Press, 1987.

Smart, James S. *The Teaching Ministry of the Church: An Examination of the Basic Principles of Christian Education.* Philadelphia: The Westminster Press, 1964.

Spitz, Lewis W. *The Renaissance and Reformation Movements,* vol. 2. *The Reformation.* Saint Lewis: Concordia Publishing House, 1971.

Stevenson, William. *The Story of the Reformation.* Richmond: John Knox Press, 1959.

Sweet, William W. *The Story of Religion in America.* Grand Rapids: Baker Book House, 1950.

Tidwell, Charles A. *Educational Ministry of a Church.* Nashville: Broadman Press, 1982.

Wilds, Elmer Harrison, and Lottich, Kenneth V. *The Foundations of Modern Education,* 4th ed. New York: Holt, Rinehart and Winston, Inc., 1970.

Wilkinson, L. P. *The Roman Experience.* New York: Alfred D. Knopf, Inc., 1974.

Articles

Clemmons, William P. "The Contributions of the Sunday School to Southern Baptist Churches." *Baptist History and Heritage* XVIII (January 1983): 31-43.

Ellison, H. L. "Sunday." In *The New International Dictionary of the Christian Church,* rev. ed., edited by J. D. Douglas, 939-40. Grand Rapids: Zondervan Press, 1978.

Fisher, Ben. C. "The Case for the Christian College." *Adult Leadership* (February 1976): 10-11.

Fitch, James E. "Major Thrusts in Sunday School Development Since 1900." In *Baptist History and Heritage* XVIII (January 1983): 17-30.

Friedrich, Otto. "What Do Babies Know?" *Time,* 15 August 1983, 52-59.

Hendricks, William L. "Stewardship in the New Testament." *Southwestern Journal of Theology* 13 (Spring 1971): 25-33.

Labouvie-Vief, Gisela. "Dynamic Development and Mature Autonomy." *Human Development* 25 (May-June 1982): 161-91.

Lake, Donald M. "Baptism." In *The New International Dictionary of the Christian Church*, rev. ed., edited by J. D. Douglas, 99-101. Grand Rapids: Zondervan Press, 1978.

McNair, Philip. "Seeds of Renewal." In *Eerdman's Handbook to the History of Christianity*, edited by Tim Dowley, 346-59. Grand Rapids: Wm. B. Eerdmans Publishing Co., 1977.

May, Lynn E. Jr. "The Sunday School: A Two-Hundred-Year Heritage." *Baptist History and Heritage* XV (October 1980): 3-11.

May, Lynn E. Jr. "The Emerging Role of Sunday Schools in Southern Baptist Life to 1900." *Baptist History and Heritage* XVIII (January 1983): 6-15.

Simpson, E. J. "The Classification of Educational Objectives in the Psychomotor Domain." *The Psychomotor Domain*, vol. 3. Washington, D.C.: Gryphon House, 1972.

Smith, Ralph L. "Old Testament Concepts of Stewardship." *Southwestern Journal of Theology* 13 (Spring 1971): 7-13.

Index